THE LIFE OF DANIEL BOONE

DANIEL BOONE

THE LIFE OF
DANIEL BOONE
The Founder of the State of Kentucky

By CECIL B. HARTLEY

WITH AN INTRODUCTION BY
G. MERCER ADAM

Fredonia Books
Amsterdam, The Netherlands

The Life of Daniel Boone:
The Founder of the State of Kentucky

And Colonel's Boones Autobiography

by
Cecil B. Hartley
and Daniel Boone

ISBN: 1-58963-990-1

Fredonia Books
Amsterdam, The Netherlands
http://www.fredoniabooks.com

PREFACE.

THE subject of the following biography, the celebrated COLONEL DANIEL BOONE, is one of the most remarkable men which this country has produced. His character is marked with originality, and his actions were important and influential in one of the most interesting periods of our history—that of the early settlement of Kentucky. Boone is generally acknowledged as the founder of that State. His having explored it alone to a considerable extent; his leading the earliest bands of settlers; his founding Boonesborough, the nucleus of the future State; his having defended this and other stations successfully against the attacks of the Indians; and the prominent part which he took in military affairs at this period of distress and peril, certainly render his claims to the distinguished honor of founding Kentucky very strong.

But Boone, personally, reaped very little benefit from his patriotic and disinterested exertions. The lands which he had first cultivated and defended, were taken from him by the chicanery of the law; other lands granted to him by the Spanish government were lost by his inattention to legal forms; and in his old age he was without an acre of land which he could call his own. A few years before his death a small tract, such as any other settler in Missouri was entitled to, was granted him by Congress. But he has left to his numerous posterity a nobler inheritance—that of an imperishable fame in the annals of his country!

CONTENTS.

CHAPTER I.

CHAPTER II.

CHAPTER III.

CHAPTER VI.

CHAPTER VII.

CHAPTER VIII.

CHAPTER IX.

CHAPTER X.

CHAPTER XI.

CHAPTER XII.

CHAPTER XIII.

CHAPTER XIV.

CONTENTS.

INTRODUCTORY NOTE.

THE story of pioneer life in the early wilds of Kentucky and "the Winning of the West"—to use President Roosevelt's apt title-phrase—is exciting and full of interest. One of its first white discoverers was the hunter, John Finley, who, in 1767, with some companions, crossed the Alleghanies and entered the hitherto little known region beyond. Of this early pioneer, Colonel Daniel Boone, then residing at Yadkin, S. C., interestingly heard, and in 1769 he and six comrade woodsmen set out across the mountains by way of Cumberland Gap to explore for themselves the Eastern Kentucky district, which in early days was known to the outer world by the now almost forgotten designation of the colony of Transylvania. Previous to this time the explorers in the region had been few; and even the Indian inhabitants had departed from it, to be afterwards harried by the troops of Lord Dunmore in the Ohio Valley in the Western border war of the Revolution.

Boone's progenitors had emigrated from Devon, England, and settled in Pennsylvania, where some of them joined the Quakers, while Boone's father, in 1748, removed to South Carolina and settled on the Yadkin at Holman's Ford. It was there that Daniel Boone set forth, as above narrated, and, though twice captured by Indians, he escaped and returned to his home in

1771, only, however, to set out again for Kentucky two years later, and this time with his family and the families of six other emigrants.

In Kentucky, Boone and his little colony built a fort on the left bank of the Kentucky River, at a place they called Boonesborough, and here they lived an exciting, adventurous life, in constant danger from lurking Indians, who once more made Boone captive, with some of his people; while two of his daughters were surprised canoeing on the river, though immediately rescued. Boone and his comrades were conveyed by the Indians to Detroit, where all were ransomed save Boone himself, who was taken to the tribal seat, Chillicothe, and there adopted into the family of a Shawnee chief. Though closely watched by his captors, Boone, on learning that the tribe contemplated a raid on his own settlement, managed to escape, and after a journey of 160 miles turned up, to the surprise of all, in time to defend his family and people in the fort from an attacking party of 450 Indians and some Frenchmen, who assailed their stronghold for over twelve days, but were finally beaten off with great loss. This determined assault on the fort of Boonesborough is described as "one of the most heroic of those bloody struggles between civilization and barbarism which have rendered the plains of Kentucky memorable." The attacking Indians, as we have said, were aided by some French, under Captain Duquesne; and both Indians and French bore British and French colors, while the surrender of the Fort was demanded in the name of His Britannic Majesty. After the raising of the siege and the departure of the assaulting force, the Fort was afterwards free from Indian attack; while settlement in Kentucky rapidly advanced, the Revolutionary War driving many settlers far to the West.

The event we have just related took place in August, 1778, and, four years later, Boone fought a battle against the Indians at Blue Licks, where one of his sons was killed. In 1790, on the separation of Kentucky from Virginia, the great hunter and pioneer settled for a time at Point Pleasant, on the Kanawha River; and from 1795 to 1804, after removing to Missouri, then a Spanish possession, he acted as Commandant of the Femme Osage district, having received a grant of 8,000 acres for his public services. This and other land grants Boone unfortunately lost when the United States became possessed of Spanish territory; though he was to some extent recouped for these losses by other land grants, after an appeal to the Legislature of Kentucky and to Congress. Boone died on his Missouri farm at Charette in September, 1820, and a quarter of a century afterwards the State of Kentucky paid his memory the honor of removing his remains for interment in Kentucky soil, near Frankfort. Here his grave is the object of veneration by the patriotic among his countrymen, and by those especially who remember his great services at an early era to what is now the State of Kentucky.

G. MERCER ADAM.

LIFE AND TIMES

OF

COLONEL DANIEL BOONE.

CHAPTER I.

The family of Daniel Boone—His grandfather emigrates to America, and settles in Bucks County, Pennsylvania—Family of Daniel Boone's father—Account of Exeter, the birthplace of Boone—Birth of Daniel Boone—Religion of his family—Boone's boyhood—Goes to School—Anecdote—Summary termination of his schooling.

THE immediate ancestors and near relations of the American Boone family, resided at Bradwinch, about eight miles from Exeter, England. George Boone, the grandfather of Daniel, emigrated to America and arrived, with Mary his wife, at Philadelphia, on the 10th of October, 1717. They brought with them eleven children, two daughters and nine sons. The names of three of the sons have come down to us.

1

John, James, and Squire. The last of these, Squire Boone, was the father of Daniel.

George Boone, immediately after his arrival in America, purchased a large tract of land in what is now Bucks County, which he settled and called it Exeter, after the city near which he was born. The records distinguish it only as the township of Exeter, without any county. He purchased also various other tracts in Maryland and Virginia; and our tradition says, among others, the ground on which Georgetown, District of Columbia, now stands, and that he laid the town out, and gave it his own name. His sons John and James lived and died on the Exeter purchase.[*]

Daniel Boone's father, Squire Boone, had seven sons and four daughters, viz.: James,[†] Samuel, Jonathan, Daniel, George, Squire, Edward, Sarah, Elizabeth, Mary, and Hannah.

Exeter Township is situated in Bucks County, Pennsylvania, and now has a population of over

[*] " Pittsburg Gazette," quoted by Peck.

[†] The eldest, James, was killed by the Indians in 1773, and his son Israel was killed at the battle of Blue Licks, August 19th. 1782.

two thousand. Here Daniel Boone was born, on the 11th of February, 1735.*

The maiden name of Boone's mother was Sarah Morgan. Some dispute has arisen respecting the religious persuasion of the Boone family. It would appear, on a review of the whole controversy, that before their removal to this country, the Boones were Episcopalians; but during their residence in Pennsylvania they permitted themselves to be considered Quakers. What sort of a Quaker Daniel Boone himself was, will be apparent in the course of our narrative.

Exeter, the native place of Daniel Boone, was at this period a small frontier settlement, consisting of log-houses, surrounded with woods, which abounded with game of various kinds and were occasionally infested with hostile Indians. It is not surprising that Daniel, passing the period of his boyhood in such a place,

* Bogant gives 11th of February, 1735. Peck, February, 1735. Another account gives 1746 as the year of his birth, and Bucks County as his birthplace. The family record, in the handwriting of Daniel Boone's uncle, James, who was a schoolmaster, gives the 14th of July, 1732.

should have acquired at an early age the ac·complishments of a hunter and woodsman. From a mere child it was his chief delight to roam in the woods, to observe the wild haunts of Nature, and to pursue the wild animals which were then so abundant.

Of the boyhood of Daniel Boone, one of his bi·ographers gives the following account. Speaking of the residence of the family at Exeter, he says :*

"Here they lived for ten years; and it was during this time that their son Daniel began to show his passion for hunting. He was scarcely able to carry a gun when he was shooting all the squirrels, raccoons, and even wild cats (it is said), that he could find in that region. As he grew older, his courage increased, and then we find him amusing himself with higher game. Other lads in the neighborhood were soon taught by him the use of the rifle, and were then able to join him in his adventures. On one occasion, they all started out for a hunt,

* " Adventures of Daniel Boone, the Kentucky Rifleman.' By the author of " Uncle Philip's Conversations."

and, after amusing themselves till it was almost dark, were returning homeward, when suddenly a wild cry was heard in the woods. The boys screamed out, 'A panther! A panther!' and ran off as fast as they could. Boone stood firmly, looking around for the animal. It was a panther indeed. His eye lighted upon him just in the act of springing toward him; in an instant he leveled his rifle, and shot him through the heart.

"But this sort of sport was not enough for him. He seemed resolved to go away from men, and live in the forests with these animals. One morning he started off as usual, with his rifle and dog. Night came on, but Daniel did not return to his home. Another day and night passed away, and still the boy did not make his appearance. His parents were now greatly alarmed. The neighbors joined them in making search for the lad. After wandering about a great while, they at length saw smoke rising from a cabin in the distance. Upon reaching it, they found the boy. The floor of the cabin was covered with the skins

of such animals as he had slain, and pieces of
meat were roasting before the fire for his
supper. Here, at a distance of three miles
from any settlement, he had built his cabin of
sods and branches and sheltered himself in the
wilderness.

"It was while his father was living on the
headwaters of the Schuylkill that young Boone
received, so far as we know, all his education.
Short indeed were his schoolboy days. It
happened that an Irish schoolmaster strolled
into the settlement, and, by the advice of Mr.
Boone and other parents, opened a school in
the neighborhood. It was not then as it is
now. Good schoolhouses were not scattered
over the land; nor were schoolmasters always
able to teach their pupils. The schoolhouse
where the boys of this settlement went was a
log-cabin, built in the midst of the woods.
The schoolmaster was a strange man; sometimes good-humored, and then indulging the
lads; sometimes surly and ill-natured, and then
beating them severely. It was his usual
custom, after hearing the first lessons of the

morning, to allow the children to be out for a half hour at play, during which time he strolled off to refresh himself from his labors. He always walked in the same direction, and the boys thought that after his return, when they were called in, he was generally more cruel than ever. They were whipped more severely, and oftentimes without any cause. They observed this, but did not know the meaning of it. One morning young Boone asked that he might go out, and had scarcely left the schoolroom when he saw a squirrel running over the trunk of a fallen tree. True to his nature, he instantly gave chase, until at last the squirrel darted into a bower of vines and branches. Boone thrust his hand in, and, to his surprise, laid hold of a bottle of whisky. This was in the direction of his master's morning walks, and he thought now that he understood the secret of much of his ill-nature. He returned to the schoolroom; but, when they were dismissed for that day, he told some of the larger boys of his discovery. Their plan was soon arranged. Early the next morning a bottle of whisky, having tartar emetic in it, was placed in the bower and the other bottle thrown away. At the usual hour, the lads were sent out to play, and the master started on his walk. But their play was to come afterward; they longed for the master to return. At length they were called in, and in a little time saw the success of their experiment. The master began to look pale and sick, yet still went on with his work. Several boys were called up, one after the other, to recite lessons, and all whipped soundly, whether right or wrong. At last young Boone was called out to answer questions in arithmetic. He came forward with his slate and pencil, and the master began. "If you subtract six from nine what remains?" said he. "Three, sir," said Boone. "Very good," said the master, "now let us come to fractions. If you take three-quarters from a whole number what remains?" The whole, sir," answered Boone. "You blockhead!" cried the master, beating him; "you stupid little fool, how can you show that?" "If I take one bottle of whisky," said Boone, "and put in its place another in which

I have mixed an emetic, the whole will remain if nobody drinks it!" The Irishman, dreadfully sick, was now doubly enraged. He seized Boone, and commenced beating him; the children shouted and roared; the scuffle continued until Boone knocked the master down upon the floor, and rushed out of the room. It was a day of freedom now for the lads. The story soon ran through the neighborhood; Boone was rebuked by his parents, but the schoolmaster was dismissed, and thus ended the boy's education.

Thus freed from school, he now returned more ardently than ever to his favorite pursuit. His dog and rifle were his constant companions, and day after day he started from home, only to roam through the forests. Hunting seemed to be the only business of his life; and he was never so happy as when at night he came home laden with game. He was an untiring wanderer."

Perhaps it was not a very serious misfortune for Daniel Boone that his school instruction was so scanty, for, "in another kind of education," says Mr. Peck,* "not unfrequent in the wilds of the West, he was an adept. No Indian could poise the rifle, find his way through the pathless forest, or search out the retreats of game, more readily than Daniel Boone. In all that related to Indian sagacity, border life, or the tactics of the skilful hunter, he excelled. The successful training of a hunter, or woodsman, is a kind of education of mental discipline, differing from that of the schoolroom, but not less effective in giving vigor to the mind, quickness of apprehension, and habits of close observation. Boone was regularly trained in all that made him a successful backwoodsman. Indolence and imbecility never produced a Simon Kenton, a Tecumthè, or a Daniel Boone. To gain the skill of an accomplished hunter requires talents, patience, perseverance, sagacity, and habits of thinking. Amongst other qualifications, knowledge of human nature, and especially of Indian character is indispensable to the pioneer of a wilderness. Add to these, self-possession, self-control, and promptness in execution. Persons

* "Life of Daniel Boone." By John M. Peck.

who are unaccustomed to a frontier residence know not how much, in the preservation of life, and in obtaining subsistence, depends on such characteristics !"

In the woods surrounding the little settlement of Exeter, Boone had ample opportunity for perfecting himself in this species of mental discipline, and of gaining that physical training of the limbs and muscles so necessary in the pursuits of the active hunter and pioneer. We have no record of his ever having encountered the Indians during his residence in Pennsylvania. His knowledge of their peculiar modes of hunting and war was to be attained not less thoroughly at a somewhat later period of life.

CHAPTER II

Removal of Boone's father and family to North Carolina—
Location on the Yadkin River—Character of the country
and the people—Byron's description of the backwoodsman—
Daniel Boone marries Rebecca Bryan—His farmer life in
North Carolina—State of the country—Political troubles
foreshadowed—Illegal fees and taxes—Probable effect of
this state of things on Boone's mind—Signs of movement.

WHEN Daniel Boone was still a youth, his father emigrated to North Carolina. The precise date of this removal of the family residence is not known. Mr. Peck, an excellent authority, says it took place when Daniel was about eighteen years old. This would make it about the year 1752.

The new residence of Squire Boone, Daniel's father, was near Holman's Ford, on the Yadkin River, about eight miles from Wilkesboro' The fact of the great backwoodsman having passed many years of his life there is still remembered with pride by the inhabitants of that region. The capital of Watauga County which

12

was formed in 1849, is named Boone, in honor of Daniel Boone. The historian of North Carolina * is disposed to claim him as a son of the State. He says: "In North Carolina Daniel Boone was reared. Here his youthful days were spent; and here that bold spirit was trained, which so fearlessly encountered the perils through which he passed in after life. His fame is part of her property, and she has inscribed his name on a town in the region where his youth was spent."

"The character of Boone is so peculiar," says Mr. Wheeler, "that it marks the age in which he lived and his name is celebrated in the verses of the immortal Byron:

> "'Of all men——
> Who passes for in life and death most lucky,
> Of the great names which in our faces stare,
> Is Daniel Boone, backwoodsman of Kentucky.
> *　　　*　　　*　　　*
> Crime came not near him—she is not the child
> Of Solitude. Health shrank not from him, for
> Her home is in the rarely-trodden wild.
> *　　　*　　　*　　　*
> And tall and strong and swift of foot are they,
> Beyond the dwarfing city's pale abortions,

* John H. Wheeler. " Historical Sketches of North Carolina.

Because their thoughts had never been the prey
Of care or gain ; the green woods were their portions.
No sinking spirits told them they grew gray,
No fashions made them apes of her distortions.
Simple they were, not savage ; and their rifles,
Though very true, were not yet used for trifles.

Motion was in their days, rest in their slumbers,
And cheerfulness the handmaid of their toil.
Not yet too many nor too few their numbers;
Corruption could not make their hearts her soil ;
The lust which stings, the splendor which encumbers,
With the free foresters divide no spoil ;
Serene, not sullen, were the solitudes
Of this unsighing people of the woods.' "

We quote these beautiful lines, because they
so aptly and forcibly describe the peculiar
character of Boone ; and to a certain extent, as
Mr. Wheeler intimates, his character was that
of his times and of his associates.

It was during the residence of the family on
the banks of the Yadkin, that Boone formed
the acquaintance of Rebecca Bryan, whom he
married.* The marriage appears, by compari-

* The children by this marriage were nine in number.
Sons : James, born in 1756, Israel, Jesse, Daniel, and Nathan.
Daughters : Susan, Jemima, Lavinia, and Rebecca.

The eldest, James, was killed, as will appear in our subsequent narrative, by the Indians, in 1773 ; and Israel fell in the
battle of Blue Licks, May 17th, 1782. In 1846, Nathan, a captain in the United States service, was the only surviving son.

son of dates, to have taken place in the year
1755. " One almost regrets," says Mr. Peck,
" to spoil so beautiful a romance as that which
has had such extensive circulation in the various 'Lives of Boone,' and which represents
him as mistaking the bright eyes of this young
lady, in the dark, for those of a deer; a mistake
that nearly proved fatal from the unerring rifle
of the young hunter. Yet, in truth, we are
bound to say, that no such mistake ever happened. Our backwoods swains never make
such mistakes."

The next five years after his marriage, Daniel
Boone passed in the quiet pursuits of a farmer's
life, varied occasionally by hunting excursions
in the woods. The most quiet and careless of
the citizens of North Carolina were not unobservant, however, of the political aspect of the
times. During this period the people, by their
representatives in the Legislature, began that
opposition to the Royal authority, which was in
after years to signalize North Carolina as one
of the leading Colonies in the Revolutionary
struggle.

The newly-appointed Royal Governor, Arthur Dobbs, arrived at Newbern in the autumn of 1754. "Governor Dobbs' administration of ten years," says the historian Wheeler, "was a continued contest between himself and the Legislature, on matters frivolous and unimportant. A high-toned temper for Royal prerogatives on his part, and an indomitable resistance of the Colonists. * * * * The people were much oppressed by Lord Grenville's agents. They seized Corbin, his agent, who lived below Edenton, and brought him to Enfield, where he was compelled to give bond and security to produce his books and disgorge his illegal fees."

This matter of illegal fees was part of a system of oppression, kindred to the famous Stamp Act—a system which was destined to grow more and more intolerable under Governor Tryon's administration, and to lead to the formation of the famous company of Regulators, whose resistance of taxation and tyranny was soon to convulse the whole State.

We are by no means to suppose that Daniel

Boone was an unobservant spectator of what was passing even at the time we are speaking of, nor that the doings of the tax-gatherers had nothing to do with his subsequent movements. He not only hated oppression, but he hated also strife and disturbance; and already began to long for a new migration into the distant woods and quiet intervales, where politics and the tax-gatherer should not intrude.

The population in his neighborhood was increasing, and new settlements were being formed along the Yadkin and its tributary streams, and explorations were made to the northwest on the banks of the Holston and Clinch rivers. The times were already beginning to exhibit symptoms of restlessness and stir among the people, which was soon to result in the formation of new States and the settlement of the far West.

CHAPTER III.

THE reader will recollect that the period referred to in the last chapter comprehended the latter years of the celebrated Seven Years' War. During the chief portion of this period, the neighboring Colony of Virginia suffered all the horrors of Indian war on its western frontier— horrors from which even the ability, courage, and patriotism of Washington were for a long time unable to protect them. The war was virtually terminated by the campaign of 1759,

18

when Quebec was taken.   The next year Canada
was ceded to England; and a Cherokee war,
which had disturbed the border settlers of North
Carolina, was terminated.   Daniel Boone's biographers all agree that it was about this time
when he first began to make long excursions
toward the West; but it is difficult to fix exactly
the date of his first long journey through the
woods in this direction.   It is generally dated
in 1771 or 1772.   We now make a quotation
from Ramsay's Annals of Tennessee, which
shows, beyond the possibility of a doubt, that
he hunted on the Wataga River in 1760, and
renders it probable that he was in the West at
an earlier date.   Our readers will excuse the
length of this quotation, as the first part of it
gives so graphic a picture of the hunter and
pioneer life of the times of Daniel Boone, and
also shows what had been done by others in
western explorations before Boone's expeditions
commenced.

  " The Colonists of the Carolinas and of Virginia had been steadily advancing to the West,
and we have traced their approaches in the direc-

tion of our eastern boundary,* to the base of
the great Appalachian range.

" Of the country beyond it, little was positively
known or accurately understood. A wandering
Indian would imperfectly delineate upon the
sand, a feeble outline of its more prominent
physical features—its magnificent rivers, with
their numerous tributaries—its lofty mountains,
its dark forests, its extended plains and its vast
extent. A voyage in a canoe, from the source
of the Hogohegee † to the Wabash, ‡ required
for its performance, in their figurative language,
" two paddles, two warriors, three moons." The
Ohio itself was but a tributary of a still larger
river, of whose source, size and direction, no in-
telligible account could be communicated or
understood. The Muscle Shoals and the ob-
structions in the river above them, were represented as mighty cataracts and fearful whirl-
pools, and the Suck, as an awful vortex. The
wild beasts with which the illimitable forests

---

* That is, the eastern boundary of Tennessee, which was
then a part of North Carolina.
† Holston.
‡ The Ohio was known many years by this name

abounded, were numbered by pointing to the leaves upon the trees, or the stars in a cloudless sky.

"These glowing descriptions of the West seemed rather to stimulate than to satisfy the intense curiosity of the approaching settlers. Information more reliable, and more minute, was, from time to time, furnished from other sources. In the Atlantic cities accounts had been received from French and Spanish traders, of the unparalleled beauty and fertility of the western interior. These reports, highly colored and amplified, were soon received and known upon the frontier. Besides, persons engaged in the interior traffic with the south-western Indian tribes had, in times of peace, penetrated their territories—traded with and resided amongst the natives—and upon their return to the white settlements, confirmed what had been previously reported in favor of the distant countries they had seen. As early as 1690, Doherty, a trader from Virginia, had visited the Cherokees and afterward lived among them a number of years. In 1730, Adair. from South Carolina,

had traveled, not only through the towns of
this tribe, but had extended his tour to most of
the nations south and west of them. He was
not only an enterprising trader but an intelligent tourist. To his observations upon the sev
eral tribes which he visited, we are indebted
for most that is known of their earlier history.
They were published in London in 1775.

"In 1740 other traders went among the
Cherokees from Virginia. They employed Mr.
Vaughan as a packman, to transport their goods.
West of Amelia County, the country was then
thinly inhabited; the last hunter's cabin that
he saw was on Otter River, a branch of the
Staunton, now in Bedford County, Va. The
route pursued was along the Great Path to the
center of the Cherokee nation. The traders
and packmen generally confined themselves to
this path till it crossed the Little Tennessee
River, then spreading themselves out among the
several Cherokee villages west of the mountain,
continued their traffic as low down the Great
Tennessee as the Indian settlements upon
Occochappo or Bear Creek, below the Muscle

Shoals, and there encountered the competition
of other traders, who were supplied from New
Orleans and Mobile. They returned, heavily
laden with peltries, to Charleston, or the more
northern markets, where they were sold at
highly remunerating prices. A hatchet, a
pocket looking-glass, a piece of scarlet cloth, a
trinket, and other articles of little value, which
at Williamsburg could be bought for a few
shillings, would command from an Indian hunter
on the Hiwasse or Tennessee peltries amounting
in value to double the number of pounds sterling. Exchanges were necessarily slow, but the
profits realized from the operation were im-
mensely large. In times of peace this traffic
attracted the attention of many adventurous
traders. It became mutually advantageous to
the Indian not less than to the white man.
The trap and the rifle, thus bartered for, procured, in one day, more game to the Cherokee
hunter than his bow and arrow and his dead-fall
would have secured during a month of toilsome
hunting. Other advantages resulted from it to
the whites. They became thus acquainted with

the great avenues leading through the hunting grounds and to the occupied country of the neighboring tribes—an important circumstance in the condition of either war or peace. Further, the traders were an exact thermometer of the pacific or hostile intention and feelings of the Indians with whom they traded. Generally, they were foreigners, most frequently Scotchmen, who had not been long in the country, or upon the frontier, who, having experienced none of the cruelties, depredations or aggressions of the Indians, cherished none of the resentment and spirit of retaliation born with, and everywhere manifested by, the American settler. Thus, free from animosity against the aborigines, the trader was allowed to remain in the village where he traded unmolested, even when its warriors were singing the war song or brandishing the war club, preparatory to an invasion or massacre of the whites. Timely warning was thus often given, by a returning packman to a feeble and unsuspecting settlement, of the perfidy and cruelty meditated against it.

"This gainful commerce was, for a time, engrossed by the traders; but the monopoly was not allowed to continue long. Their rapid accumulations soon excited the cupidity of another class of adventurers; and the hunter, in his turn, became a co-pioneer with the trader, in the march of civilization to the wilds of the West. As the agricultural population approached the eastern base of the Alleghanies, the game became scarce, and was to be found by severe toil in almost inaccessible recesses and coves of the mountain. Packmen, returning from their trading expeditions, carried with them evidences, not only of the abundance of game across the mountains, but of the facility with which it was procured. Hunters began to accompany the traders to the Indian towns; but, unable to brook the tedious delay of procuring peltries by traffic, and impatient of restraint, they struck boldly into the wilderness and western-like, to use a western phrase, set up for themselves. The reports of their return, and of their successful enterprise, stimulated other adventurers to a similar undertaking. 'As early as 1748

Doctor Thomas Walker, of Virginia, in company with Colonels Wood, Patton and Buchanan, and Captain Charles Campbell, and a number of hunters, made an exploring tour upon the western waters. Passing Powell's valley, he gave the name of "Cumberland" to the lofty range of mountains on the west. Tracing this range in a southwestern direction, he came to a remarkable depression in the chain: through this he passed, calling it "Cumberland Gap." On the western side of the range he found a beautiful mountain stream, which he named "Cumberland River," all in honor of the Duke of Cumberland, then prime minister of England.' * These names have ever since been retained, and, with Loudon, are believed to be the only names in Tennessee of English origin.

"Although Fort Loudon was erected as early as 1756 upon the Tennessee, yet it was in advance of any white settlements nearly one hundred and fifty miles, and was destroyed in 1760. The fort, too, at Long Island, within the bound-

---

* Monette. The Indian name of this range was Wasioto, and of the river, Shawnee.

aries of the present State of Tennessee, were erected in 1758, but no permanent settlements had yet been formed near it. Still occasional settlers had begun to fix their habitations in the southwestern section of Virginia, and as early as 1754, six families were residing west of New River. 'On the breaking out of the French war, the Indians, in alliance with the French, made an irruption into these settlements, and massacred Burke and his family. The other families, finding their situation too perilous to be maintained, returned to the eastern side of New River; and the renewal of the attempt to carry the white settlements further west was not made until after the close of that war.' *

"Under a mistaken impression that the Virginia line, when extended west, would embrace it, a grant of land was this year made, by the authorities of Virginia, to Edmund Pendleton, for three thousand acres of land, lying in Augusta County on a branch of the middle fork of the Indian river called

1756 {

* Howe.

West Creek,* now Sullivan County, Tennessee.

"In this year Doctor Walker again passed over
1760 { Clinch and Powell's River, on a tour of exploration into what is now Kentucky.

"The Cherokees were now at peace with the
whites and hunters from the back settlements
began with safety to penetrate deeper and further
1761 { into the wilderness of Tennessee. Several of them, chiefly from Virginia,
hearing of the abundance of game with which
the woods were stocked, and allured by the
prospects of gain, which might be drawn from
this source, formed themselves into a company,
composed of Wallen, Scaggs, Blevins, Cox, and
fifteen others, and came into the valley since
known as Carter's Valley, in Hawkins County,
Tennessee. They hunted eighteen months upon
Clinch and Powell's Rivers. Wallen's Creek
and Wallen's Ridge received their name from
the leader of the company; as also did the

* The original patent, signed by Governor Dinwiddie, and
now in the possession of the writer, was presented to him by
T. A. R. Nelson, Esq., of Jonesboro, Tennessee. It is probably the oldest grant in the state.

station which they erected in the present Lee County, Virginia, the name of Wallen's station. They penetrated as far north as Laurel Mountain, in Kentucky, where they terminated their journey, having met with a body of Indians, whom they supposed to be Shawnees. At the head of one of the companies that visited the West this year 'came Daniel Boon, from the Yadkin, in North Carolina, and traveled with them as low as the place where Abingdon now stands, and there left them.'

"This is the first time the advent of Daniel Boon to the western wilds has been mentioned by historians, or by the several biographers of that distinguished pioneer and hunter. There is reason, however, to believe that he had hunted upon Watauga earlier. The writer is indebted to N. Gammon, Esq., formerly of Jonesboro, now a citizen of Knoxville, for the following inscription, still to be seen upon a beech tree, standing in sight and east of the present stage-road, leading from Jonesboro to Blountsville, and in the valley of Boon's Creek, a tributary of Watauga:

                            D Boon
CillED   *A. BAR*   *On*
                                            Tree
in   *ThE*
yEAR
                            1760

" Boon was eighty-six years old when he
died, which was September, 1820. He was
thus twenty-six years old when the inscription
was made.   When he left the company of
hunters in 1761, as mentioned above by Hay-
wood, it is probable that he did so to revisit
the theater of a former hunt upon the creek
that still bears his name, and where his camp is
still pointed out near its banks.   It is not im-
probable, indeed, that he belonged to, or accompanied, the party of Doctor Walker, on his
first, or certainly on his second, tour of exploration in 1760.   The inscription is sufficient authority, as this writer conceives, to date the
arrival of Boon in Tennessee as early as its
date, 1760 thus preceding the permanent settlement of the country nearly ten years."

It will be observed that the historian in this

extract spells Boon without the final *e*, following the orthography of the hunter, in his inscription on the tree. This orthography Boone
used at a later period, as we shall show. But
the present received mode of spelling the name
is the one which we have adopted in this work.

On a subsequent page of Wheeler's history,
we find the following memorandum:

"Daniel Boon, who still lived on the Yadkin,
though he had previously hunted on the Western waters, came again this year to explore the
country, being employed for this purpose by
Henderson & Company. With him came
Samuel Callaway, his kinsman, and the ancestor
of the respectable family of that name, pioneers
of Tennessee, Kentucky and Missouri. Callaway
was at the side of Boon when approaching the
spurs of the Cumberland Mountain, and in view
of the vast herds of buffalo grazing in the valleys
between them, he exclaimed, "I am richer than
the man mentioned in Scripture, who owned
the cattle on a thousand hills; I own the wild
beasts of more than a thousand valleys."

After Boone and Callaway, came another

hunter, Henry Scaggins, who was also employed by Henderson. He extended his explorations to the Lower Cumberland, and fixed his station at Mansco's Lick.

We shall have occasion to speak more particularly of Henderson's company and Boone's connection with it; but we will first call the reader's attention to the state of affairs in North Carolina at this period, and their probable influence on the course pursued by Daniel Boone.

CHAPTER IV.

THERE were many circumstances in the social
and political condition of the State of North
Carolina during the period of Daniel Boone's
residence on the banks of the Yadkin, which
were calculated to render him restless and
quite willing to seek a home in the Western
wilderness. Customs and fashions were chang-
ing. The Scotch traders, to whom we have

3   33

referred in the last chapter, and others of the
same class, were introducing an ostentatious
and expensive style of living, quite inappropriate to the rural population of the colony.
In dress and equipage, they far surpassed the
farmers and planters; and they were not back-
ward in taking upon themselves airs of superiority on this account. In this they were imitated
by the officers and agents of the Royal government of the colony, who were not less fond of
luxury and show. To support their extrava-
gant style of living these minions of power,
magistrates, lawyers, clerks of court, and tax-
gatherers, demanded exorbitant fees for their
services. The Episcopal clergy, supported by
a legalized tax on the people, were not content
with their salaries, but charged enormous fees
for the occasional services. A fee of fifteen
dollars was exacted from the poor farmer for
performing the marriage service. The collection of taxes was enforced by suits at law, with
enormous expense; and executions, levies, and
distresses were of every-day occurrence. All
sums exceeding forty shillings were sued for

and executions obtained in the courts, the original debt being saddled with extortionate bills of cost. Sheriffs demanded more than was due, under threats of sheriff's sales; and they applied the gains thus made to their own use. Money, as is always the case in a new country, was exceedingly scarce, and the sufferings of the people were intolerable.

Petitions to the Legislature for a redress of grievances were treated with contempt. The people assembled and formed themselves into an association for *regulating* public grievances and abuse of power. Hence the name given to them of Regulators. They resolved "to pay only such taxes as were agreeable to law and applied to the purpose therein named, to pay no officer more than his legal fees." The subsequent proceedings of the Regulators, such as forcible resistance to officers and acts of personal violence toward them, at length brought on an actual collision between them and an armed force led by the Royal Governor, Tryon (May 16, 1771,) at Alamanance, in which the Regulators were defeated; and the grievances con-

tinued with scarcely abated force till the Revolu·
tion brought relief.

Under these circumstances, it is not surpris·
ing that Daniel Boone and others were quite
willing to migrate to the West, if it were only
to enjoy a quiet life ; the dangers of Indian ag·
gression being less dreaded than the visits of
the tax-gatherer and the sheriff ; and the solitude
of the forest and prairie being preferred to the
society of insolent foreigners, flaunting in the
luxury and ostentation purchased by the spoils
of fraud and oppression.

Among the hunters and traders who pursued
their avocations in the Western wilds was John
Finley, or Findley, who led a party of hunters
in 1767 to the neighborhood of the Louisa
River, as the Kentucky River was then called,
and spent the season in hunting and trapping.
On his return, he visited Daniel Boone, and
gave him a most glowing description of the
country which he had visited—a country abound·
ing in the richest and most fertile land, inter·
sected by noble rivers, and teeming with herds
of deer and buffaloes and numerous flocks of

wild turkeys, to say nothing of the smaller game. To these descriptions Boone lent a willing ear. He resolved to accompany Finley in his next hunting expedition, and to see this terrestrial paradise with his own eyes, doubtless with the intention of ultimately seeking a home in that delightful region.

Accordingly, a company of six persons was formed for a new expedition to the West, and Boone was chosen as leader. The names of the other members of this party were John Finley, John Stuart, Joseph Holden, James Moncey, and William Cool.

Much preparation seems to have been required. Boone's wife, who was one of the best of housekeepers and managers, had to fit out his clothes, and to make arrangements for housekeeping during his expected long absence. His sons were now old enough to assist their mother in the management of the farm, but, doubtless, they had to be supplied with money and other necessaries before the father could venture to leave home; so that it was not till the 1st of May, 1769, that the party were able to set out, as Boone, in his autobiography, expresses it, " in quest of the country of Kentucky."

It was more than a month before these adventurers came in sight of the promised land. We quote from Mr. Peck's excellent work the description which undoubtedly formed the authority on which the artist has relied in painting the accompanying engraving of "Daniel Boone's first view of Kentucky." It is as follows:

" It was on the 7th of June, 1769, that six men, weary and wayworn, were seen winding their way up the steep side of a rugged mountain in the wilderness of Kentucky. Their dress was of the description usually worn at that period by all forest rangers. The outside garment was a hunting shirt, or loose open frock, made of dressed deer skins. Leggings or drawers, of the same material, covered the lower extremities, to which was appended a pair of moccasins for the feet. The cape or collar of the hunting shirt, and the seams of the leggings, were adorned with fringes. The under garments were of coarse cotton. A leather belt

encircled the body; on the right side was suspended the tomahawk, to be used as a hatchet;
on the left side was the hunting-knife, powder
horn, bullet-pouch, and other appendages indispensable for a hunter. Each person bore his
trusty rifle; and, as the party slowly made their
toilsome way amid the shrubs, and over the logs
and loose rocks that accident had thrown into
the obscure trail which they were following,
each man kept a sharp look-out, as though
danger or a lurking enemy was near. Their
garments were soiled and rent, the unavoidable
result of long traveling and exposure to the
heavy rains that had fallen; for the weather
had been stormy and most uncomfortable, and
they had traversed a mountainous wilderness for
several hundred miles. The leader of the party
was of full size, with a hardy, robust, sinewy
frame, and keen, piercing hazel eyes, that glanced
with quickness at every object as they passed
on, now cast forward in the direction they were
traveling for signs of an old trail, and in the
next moment directed askance into the dense
thicket, or into the deep ravine, as if watching

some concealed enemy. The reader will recognize in this man the pioneer Boone, at the head of his companions.

"Toward the time of the setting sun, the party had reached the summit of the mountain range, up which they had toiled for some three or four hours, and which had bounded their prospect to the west during the day. Here new and indescribable scenery opened to their view. Before them, for an immense distance, as if spread out on a map, lay the rich and beautiful vales watered by the Kentucky River; for they had now reached one of its northern branches. The country immediately before them, to use a Western phrase, was 'rolling,' and, in places, abruptly hilly; but far in the vista was seen a beautiful expanse of level country, over which the buffalo, deer, and other forest animals roamed unmolested while they fed on the luxuriant herbage of the forest. The countenances of the party lighted up with pleasure, congratulations were exchanged, the romantic tales of Finley were confirmed by ocular demonstration, and orders were given to encamp for the night in a neighboring ravine. In a deep gorge of the mountain a large tree had fallen, surrounded with a dense thicket, and hidden from observation by the abrupt and precipitous hills. This tree lay in a convenient position for the back of their camp. Logs were placed on the right and left, leaving the front open, where fire might be kindled against another log; and for shelter from the rains and heavy dews, bark was peeled from the linden trees."

This rude structure appears to have been the headquarters of the hunters through the whole summer and autumn, till late in December. During this time they hunted the deer, the bear, and especially the buffalo. The buffaloes were found in great numbers, feeding on the leaves of the cane, and the rich and spontaneous fields of clover.

During this long period they saw no Indians. That part of the country was not inhabited by any tribe at that time, although it was used occasionally as a hunting ground by the Shaw-anese, the Cherokees and the Chickesaws. The land at that time belonged to the colony of

Virginia, which then included what is now called Kentucky. The title to the ground was acquired by a treaty with the Indians, Oct. 5th, 1770. The Iroquois, at the treaty of Fort Stanwix, in 1768, had already ceded their doubtful claim to the land south of the Ohio River, to Great Britain; so that Boone's company of hunters were not trespassing upon Indian territory at this time.* But they were destined nevertheless to be treated as intruders.

On the 22d of December, Boone and John Stuart, one of his companions, left their encampment, and following one of the numerous paths which the buffalo had made through the cane, they plunged boldly into the interior of the forest. They had as yet, as we have already stated, seen no Indians, and the country had been reported as totally uninhabited. This was true in a strict sense, for although, as we have seen, the southern and northwestern tribes were in the habit of hunting here as upon neutral ground, yet not a single wigwam had been

* Peck. Life of Boone.

erected, nor did the land bear the slightest mark of having ever been cultivated.

The different tribes would fall in with each other, and from the fierce conflicts which generally followed these casual rencounters, the country had been known among them by the name of "*the dark and bloody ground!*"

The two adventurers soon learned the additional danger to which they were exposed. While roving carelessly from canebrake to canebrake, and admiring the rank growth of vegetation, and the variety of timber which marked the fertility of the soil, they were suddenly alarmed by the appearance of a party of Indians, who, springing from their place of concealment, rushed upon them with a rapidity which rendered escape impossible.

They were almost instantly seized, disarmed, and made prisoners. Their feelings may be readily imagined. They were in the hands of an enemy who knew no alternative between adoption and torture; and the numbers and fleetness of their captors rendered escape by open means impossible, while their jealous vigilance seemed equally fatal to any secret attempt.

Boone, however, was possessed of a temper admirably adapted to the circumstances in which he was placed. Of a cold and saturnine, rather than an ardent disposition, he was never either so much elevated by good fortune or depressed by bad, as to lose for an instant the full possession of all his faculties. He saw that immediate escape was impossible, but he encouraged his companion, and constrained himself to accompany the Indians in all their excursions, with so calm and contented an air, that their vigilance insensibly began to relax.

On the seventh evening of their captivity, they encamped in a thick canebrake, and having built a large fire, lay down to rest. The party whose duty it was to watch were weary and negligent, and about midnight Boone, who had not closed an eye, ascertained, from the deep breathing all around him, that the whole party, including Stuart, was in a deep sleep.

Gently and gradually extricating himself from the Indians who lay around him, he walked cautiously to the spot where Stuart lay, and having succeeded in awakening him, without alarming the rest, he briefly informed him of his determination, and exhorted him to arise, make no noise, and follow him. Stuart, although ignorant of the design, and suddenly roused from sleep, fortunately obeyed with equal silence and celerity, and within a few minutes they were beyond hearing.

Rapidly traversing the forest, by the light of the stars and the bark of the trees, they ascertained the direction in which the camp lay, but upon reaching it on the next day, to their great grief, they found it plundered and deserted, with nothing remaining to show the fate of their companions; and even to the day of his death, Boone knew not whether they had been killed or taken, or had voluntarily abandoned their cabin and returned.*

Indeed it has never been ascertained what became of Finley and the rest of Boone's party of hunters. If Finley himself had returned to Carolina, so remarkable a person would un-

* McClung. "Western Adventures."

doubtedly have left some trace of himself in the history of his time; but no trace exists of any of the party who were left at the old camp by Boone and Stuart. Boone and Stuart resumed their hunting, although their ammunition was running low, and they were compelled, by the now well-known danger of Indian hostilities, to seek for more secret and secure hiding-places at night than their old encampment in the ravine.

The only kind of firearms used by the backwoods hunter is the rifle. In the use of this weapon Boone was exceedingly skilful. The following anecdote, related by the celebrated naturalist, Audubon,* shows that he retained his wonderful precision of aim till a late period of his life.

"Barking off squirrels is delightful sport, and, in my opinion, requires a greater degree of accuracy than any other. I first witnessed this manner of procuring squirrels whilst near the town of Frankfort. The performer was the celebrated Daniel Boone. We walked out together, and followed the rocky margins of the

---

* Ornithological Biography, pp. 293-4.

Kentucky River, until we reached a piece of flat land thickly covered with black walnuts, oaks, and hickories. As the general mast was a good one that year, squirrels were seen gamboling on every tree around us. My companion, a stout, hale, and athletic man, dressed in a home spun hunting-shirt, bare-legged and moccasined, carried a long and heavy rifle which, as he was loading it, he said had proved efficient in all his former undertakings, and which he hoped would not fail on this occasion, as he felt proud to show me his skill. The gun was wiped, the powder measured, the ball patched with six-hundred-thread linen, and the charge sent home with a hickory rod. We moved not a step from the place, for the squirrels were so numerous that it was unnecessary to go after them. Boone pointed to one of these animals which had observed us, and was crouched on a branch about fifty paces distant, and bade me mark well the spot where the ball should hit. He raised his piece gradually, until the *bead* (that being the name given by the Kentuckians to the *sight*) of the barrel was brought to a line with the spot

which he intended to hit. The whip-like report resounded through the woods and along
the hills in repeated echoes. Judge of my sur
prise, when I perceived that the ball had hit
the piece of the bark immediately beneath the
squirrel, and shivered it into splinters, the con-
cussion produced by which had killed the animal, and sent it whirling through the air, as if
it had been blown up by the explosion of a
powder magazine.   Boone kept up his firing,
and before many hours had elapsed we had procured as many squirrels as we wished; for you
must know that to load a rifle requires only a
moment, and that if it is wiped once after each
shot, it will do duty for hours.   Since that first
interview with our veteran Boone, I have seen
many other individuals perform the same feat."

CHAPTER V.

In the early part of the month of January,
1776, Boone and Stuart were agreeably surprised by the arrival of Squire Boone, the
younger brother of Daniel, accompanied by
another man, whose name has not been handed
down. The meeting took place as they were
hunting in the woods. The newcomers were
hailed at a distance with the usual greeting,
" Holloa! strangers, who are you?" to which
they answered, " White men and friends."

49

And friends indeed they were—friends in need;
for they brought a supply of ammunition and
news from Daniel Boone's home and family on
the Yadkin. They had had a weary journey
through the wilderness, and although they had
met with no Indians on their way, they had
frequently come upon their traces in passing
through the woods. Their purpose in undertaking this formidable journey had been to
learn the fate of Boone and his party, whose
safety was nearly despaired of by his friends in
North Carolina, to hunt for themselves, and to
convey a supply of ammunition to Boone. It
is difficult to conceive the joy with which their
opportune arrival was welcomed. They informed Boone that they had just seen the last
night's encampment of Stuart and himself, so
that the joyful meeting was not wholly unan-
ticipated by them.

Thus reinforced, the party, now consisting of
four skilful hunters, might reasonably hope for
increased security, and a fortunate issue to their
protracted hunting tour. But they hunted in
separate parties, and in one of these Daniel

Boone and Stuart fell in with a party of Indians, who fired upon them. Stuart was shot dead and scalped by the Indians, but Boone escaped in the forest, and rejoined his brother and the remaining hunter of the party.

A few days afterward this hunter was lost in the woods, and did not return as usual to the camp. Daniel and Squire made a long and anxious search for him; but it was all in vain. Years afterward a skeleton was discovered in the woods, which was supposed to be that of the lost hunter.

The two brothers were thus left in the wilderness alone, separated by several hundred miles from home, surrounded by hostile Indians, and destitute of everything but their rifles. After having had such melancholy experience of the dangers to which they were exposed, we would naturally suppose that their fortitude would have given way, and that they would instantly have returned to the settlements. But the most remarkable feature in Boone's character was a calm and cold equanimity which rarely rose to enthusiasm and never sunk to despondence.

His courage undervalued the danger to which
he was exposed, and his presence of mind, which
never forsook him, enabled him on all occasions
to take the best means of avoiding it. The
wilderness, with all its dangers and privations,
had a charm for him, which is scarcely conceiv-
able by one brought up in a city, and he determined to remain alone while his brother returned
to Carolina for an additional supply of ammunition, as their original supply was nearly exhausted. His situation we should now suppose
in the highest degree gloomy and dispiriting
The dangers which attended his brother on
his return were nearly equal to his own; and
each had left a wife and children, which
Boone acknowledged cost him many an anxious
thought.

But the wild and solitary grandeur of the
country around him, where not a tree had been
cut, nor a house erected, was to him an inexhaustible source of admiration and delight; and
he says to himself, that some of the most rapt-
urous moments of his life were spent in those
lonely rambles. The utmost caution was neces

sary to avoid the savages, and scarcely less to escape the ravenous hunger of the wolves that prowled nightly around him in immense numbers. He was compelled frequently to shift his lodging, and by undoubted signs saw that the Indians had repeatedly visited his hut during his absence. He sometimes lay in canebrakes without fire, and heard the yells of the Indians around him. Fortunately, however, he never encountered them.*

Mr. Perkins, in his Annals of the West, speaking of this sojourn of the brothers in the wilderness, says: And now commenced that most extraordinary life on the part of these two men which has, in a great measure, served to give celebrity to their names; we refer to their residence, entirely alone, for more than a year in a land filled with the most subtle and unsparing enemies, and under the influence of no other motive, apparently, than a love of adventure, of Nature, and of solitude. Nor were they, during this time, always together. For three months, Daniel remained amid the forest utterly

* McClung.

by himself, while his brother, with courage and capacity equal to his own, returned to North Carolina for a supply of powder and lead; with which he succeeded in rejoining the roamer of the wilderness in safety in July, 1770.

It is almost impossible to conceive of the skill, coolness, and sagacity which enabled Daniel Boone to spend so many weeks in the midst of the Indians, and yet be undiscovered by them. He appears to have changed his position continually—to have explored the whole center of what forms now the State of Kentucky, and in so doing must have exposed himself to many different parties of the natives. A reader of Mr. Cooper's Last of the Mohicans may comprehend, in some measure, the arts by which he was preserved, but, after all, a natural gift seems to lie at the basis of such consummate wood-craft; an instinct, rather than any exercise of intellect, appears to have guided Boone in such matters, and made him pre-eminent among those who were most accomplished in the knowledge of forest life. Then we are to remember the week's captivity of the previous year; it was the first practical acquaintance that the pioneer had with the Western Indians, and we may be assured he spent that week in noting carefully the whole method of his captors. Indeed, we think it probable he remained in captivity so long that he might learn their arts, stratagems, and modes of concealment. We are, moreover, to keep in mind this fact: the woods of Kentucky were at that period filled with a species of nettle of such a character that, being once bent down, it did not recover itself, but remained prostrate, thus retaining the impression of a foot almost like snow—even a turkey might be tracked in it with perfect ease. This weed Boone would carefully avoid, but the natives, numerous and fearless, would commonly pay no regard to it, so that the white hunter was sure to have palpable signs of the presence of his enemies, and the direction they had taken. Considering these circumstances, it is even more remarkable that his brother should have returned in safety, with his loaded horses, than that he remained alone unharmed; though in the escape of both from captivity or death from

January, 1770, until their return to the Atlantic rivers in March, 1771, there is something so wonderful that the old pioneer's phrase, that he was "an instrument ordained to settle the wilderness," seems entirely proper.

Daniel Boone's own account of this period of his life, contained in his autobiography, is highly characteristic. It is as follows:

" Thus situated, many hundred miles from our families in the howling wilderness, I believe few would have equally enjoyed the happiness we experienced. I often observed to my brother, ' You see now how little nature requires to be satisfied. Felicity, the companion of content, is rather found in our own breasts than in the enjoyment of external things; and I firmly believe it requires but a little philosophy to make a man happy in whatsoever state he is. This consists in a full resignation to Providence, and a resigned soul finds pleasure in a path strewed with briers and thorns.'

" We continued not in a state of indolence, but hunted every day, and prepared a little cottage to defend us from the winter storms. We remained there undisturbed during the winter; and on the first of May, 1770, my brother returned home to the settlement by himself for a new recruit of horses and ammunition, leaving me by myself, without bread, salt, or sugar, without company of my fellow-creatures, or even a horse or dog. I confess I never before was under greater necessity of exercising philosophy and fortitude. A few days I passed uncomfortably. The idea of a beloved wife and family, and their anxiety on account of my absence and exposed situation, made sensible impressions on my heart. A thousand dreadful apprehensions presented themselves to my view, and had undoubtedly disposed me to melancholy if further indulged.

"One day I undertook a tour through the country, and the diversity and beauties of Nature I met with in this charming season expelled every gloomy and vexatious thought. Just at the close of day the gentle gales retired, and left the place to the disposal of a profound calm. Not a breeze shook the most tremulous leaf. I had gained the summit of a commanding ridge, and, looking round with astonishing delight, beheld the ample plains, the beauteous tracts below. On the other hand, I surveyed the famous river Ohio that rolled in silent dignity, marking the western boundary of Kentucky with inconceivable grandeur. At a vast distance I beheld the mountains lift their venerable brows, and penetrate the clouds. All things were still. I kindled a fire near a fountain of sweet water, and feasted on the loin of a buck, which a few hours before I had killed. The fallen shades of night soon overspread the whole hemisphere, and the earth seemed to gape after the hovering moisture. My roving excursion this day had fatigued my body, and diverted my imagination. I laid me down to sleep, and I awoke not until the sun had chased away the night. I continued this tour, and in a few days explored a considerable part of the country, each day equally pleased as the first. I returned to my old camp, which was not disturbed in my absence. I did not confine my lodging to it, but often reposed in thick canebrakes to avoid the savages, who, I believe, often visited my

camp, but fortunately for me in my absence.
In this situation I was constantly exposed to
danger and death. How unhappy such a situation for a man tormented with fear, which is
vain if no danger comes, and, if it does, only
augments the pain. It was my happiness to be
destitute of this afflicting passion, with which
I had the greatest reason to be affected. The
prowling wolves diverted my nocturnal hours
with perpetual howlings; and the various species
of animals in this vast forest in the daytime
were continually in my view.

" Thus I was surrounded with plenty in the
midst of want. I was happy in the midst of
dangers and inconveniences. In such a diversity it was impossible I should be disposed to
melancholy. No populous city, with all the
varieties of commerce and stately structures,
could afford so much pleasure to my mind as
the beauties of Nature I found here.

"Thus, through an uninterrupted scene of
sylvan pleasures, I spent the time until the 27th
day of July following, when my brother, to my
great felicity, met me according to appointment,

at our old camp. Shortly after we left this place, not thinking it safe to stay there any longer, and proceeded to Cumberland River, reconnoitering that part of the country until March, 1771, and giving names to the different waters.

"Soon after, I returned home to my family, with a determination to bring them as soon as possible to live in Kentucky, which I esteemed a second paradise, at the risk of my life and fortune.

"I returned safe to my old habitation, and found my family in happy circumstances."

This extract is taken from the autobiography of Daniel Boone, written from his own dictation by John Filson, and published in 1784. Some writers have censured this production as inflated and bombastic. To us it seems simple and natural; and we have no doubt that the very words of Boone are given for the most part. The use of glowing imagery and strong figures is by no means confined to highly-educated persons. Those who are illiterate, as Boone certainly was, often indulge in this style. Even

the Indians are remarkably fond of bold meta-
phors and other rhetorical figures, as is abundantly proved by their speeches and legends.

While Boone had been engaged in his late
hunting tour, other adventurers were examin-
ing the rich lands south of the Ohio.* Even in
1770, while Boone was wandering solitary in
those Kentucky forests, a band of forty hunters,
led by Colonel James Knox, had gathered from
the valleys of New River, Clinch, and Holston,
to chase the buffaloes of the West; nine of the
forty had crossed the mountains, penetrated the
desert and almost impassable country about the
heads of the Cumberland, and explored the region on the borders of Kentucky and Tennessee.
This hunting party, from the length of time it
was absent, is known in the traditions of the
West as the party of the Long Hunters. While
these bold men were penetrating the valley of
the Ohio, in the region of the Cumberland Gap,
others came from Virginia and Pennsylvania, by
the river; among them, and in the same year
that the Long Hunters were abroad (1770)

* Perkins. "Annals of the West."

came no less noted a person than George Washington. His attention, as we have before said, had been turned to the lands along the Ohio, at a very early period ; he had himself large claims, as well as far-reaching plans of settlement, and he wished with his own eyes to examine the Western lands, especially those about the mouth of the Kanawha. From the journal of his expedition, published by Mr. Sparks, in the Appendix to the second volume of his Washington Papers, we learn some valuable facts in reference to the position of affairs in the Ohio valley at that time. We learn, for instance, that the Virginians were rapidly surveying and settling the lands south of the river as far down as the Kanawhas ; and that the Indians, notwithstanding the treaty of Fort Stanwix, were jealous and angry at this constant invasion of their hunting-grounds.

"This jealousy and anger were not supposed to cool during the years next succeeding, and when Thomas Bullitt and his party descended the Ohio in the summer of 1773, he found that no settlements would be tolerated south of the river, unless the Indian hunting-grounds were left undisturbed. To leave them undisturbed was, however, no part of the plan of these white men.

"This very party, which Bullitt led, and in which were the two McAfees, Hancock, Taylor, Drennon and others, separated, and while part went up the Kentucky River, explored the banks, and made important surveys, including the valley in which Frankfort stands, the remainder went on to the Falls, and laid out, in behalf of John Campbell and John Connolly, the plan of Louisville. All this took place in the summer of 1773; and in the autumn of that year, or early in the next, John Floyd, the deputy of Colonel William Preston, the surveyor of Fincastle County, Virginia, in which it was claimed that Kentucky was comprehended, also crossed the mountains, while General Thompson, of Pennsylvania, made surveys upon the north fork of the Licking. When Boone, therefore, in September, commenced his march for the West (as we shall presently relate), the choice regions which he had examined three years before were known

to numbers, and settlers were preparing to dese-
crate the silent and beautiful woods. Nor did
the prospects of the English colonists stop with
the settlements of Kentucky. In 1773, General
Lyman, with a number of military adventurers,
went to Natchez and laid out several townships
in that vicinity; to which point emigration set
so strongly, that we are told four hundred
families passed down the Ohio on their way
thither, during six weeks of the summer of that
year." *

* Perkins. "Annals of the West."

CHAPTER VI.

DANIEL BOONE had now returned to his home on the banks of the Yadkin, after an absence of no less than two years, during which time he had not tasted, as he remarks in his autobiography, either salt, sugar, or bread. He must have enjoyed, in no ordinary degree, the comforts of home. Carolina, however, was to be his home but for a short time. He had fully determined to go with his family to Kentucky and settle in that lovely region. He was destined to found a State.

After Boone's return to North Carolina, more than two years passed away before he could complete the arrangements necessary for removing his family to Kentucky. He sold his farm

5

on the Yadkin, which had been for many years
under cultivation, and no doubt brought him
a sum amply sufficient for the expenses of his
journey and the furnishing of a new home in
the promised land. He had, of course, to over-
come the natural repugnance of his wife and
children to leave the home which had become
dear to them; and he had also to enlist other
adventurers to accompany him. And here we
deem it proper, before entering upon the account
of his departure, to quote from a cotemporary,*
some general remarks on the character of the
early settlers of Kentucky.

"Throughout the United States, generally, the
most erroneous notions prevail with respect to
the character of the first settlers of Kentucky;
and by several of the American novelists, the
most ridiculous uses have been made of the fine
materials for fiction which lie scattered over
nearly the whole extent of that region of daring
adventure and romantic incident. The common
idea seems to be, that the first wanderers to
Kentucky were a simple, ignorant, low-bred,

* W. D. Gallagher, " Hesperian," Vol. II., p. 89

good-for-nothing set of fellows, who left the frontiers and sterile places of the old States, where a considerable amount of labor was necessary to secure a livelihood, and sought the new and fertile country southeast of the Ohio River and northwest of the Cumberland Mountains, where corn would produce bread for them with simply the labor of planting, and where the achievements of their guns would supply them with meat and clothing ; a set of men who, with that instinct which belongs to the beaver, built a number of log cabins on the banks of some secluded stream, which they surrounded with palisades for the better protection of their wives and children, and then went wandering about, with guns on their shoulders, or traps under their arms, leading a solitary, listless, *ruminating* life, till aroused by the appearance of danger, or a sudden attack from unseen enemies, when instantly they approved themselves the bravest of warriors, and the most expert of strategists. The romancers who have attempted to describe their habits of life and delineate their characters, catching this last idea, and imagining things probable of the country they were in, have drawn the one in lines the most grotesque and absurd, and colored the other with a pencil dipped in all hues but the right. To them the early pioneers appear to have been people of a character demi-devil, demi-savage, not only without the remains of former civilization, but without even the recollection that they had been born and bred where people were, at the least, measurably sane, somewhat religiously inclined, and, for the most, civilly behaved.

"Both of these conceptions of the character of the Pioneer Fathers are, to a certain extent, correct as regards *individuals* among them; but the pictures which have often been given us, even when held up beside such *individuals*, will prove to be exaggerations in more respects than one. Daniel Boone is an individual instance of a man plunging into the depths of an unknown wilderness, shunning rather than seeking contact with his kind, his gun and trap the only companions of his solitude, and wandering about thus for months.

' No mark upon the tree, nor print, nor track,
To lead him forward, or to guide him back,'

contented and happy ; yet, for all this, if those
who knew him well had any true conception of
his character, Boone was a man of ambition,
and shrewdness, and energy, and fine social
qualities, and extreme sagacity. And individual instances there *may* have been—though
even this possibility is not sustained by the
primitive histories of those times—of men who
were so far *outre* to the usual course of their
kind, as to have afforded originals for the *Sam
Huggs*, the *Nimrod Wildfires*, the *Ralph Stack-
poles*, the *Tom Bruces*, and the *Earthquakes*,
which so abound in most of those fictions whose
locale is the Western country. But that naturalist who should attempt, by ever so minute a
description of a pied blackbird, to give his readers
a correct idea of the *Gracula Ferruginea* of orni-
thologists, would not more utterly fail of accomplishing his object, than have the authors whose
creations we have named, by delineating such
individual instances—by holding up, as it were,
such *outre* specimens of an original class—failed

to convey anything like an accurate impression of the habits, customs, and general character of the Western pioneers.

"Daniel Boone, and those who accompanied him into the wildernesses of Kentucky, had been little more than hunters in their original homes, on the frontiers of North Carolina; and, with the exception of their leader, but little more than hunters did they continue after their emigration. The most glowing accounts of the beauty and fertility of the country northwest of the Laurel Ridge, had reached their ears from Finley and his companions; and they shouldered their guns, strapped their wallets upon their backs and wandered through the Cumberland Gap into the dense forests, and thick brakes, and beautiful plains which soon opened upon their visions, more to indulge a habit of roving, and gratify an excited curiosity, than from any other motive; and, arrived upon the head-waters of the Kentucky, they built themselves rude log cabins, and spent most of their lives in hunting and eating, and fighting marauding bands of Indians. Of a similar character were the earliest Virginians, who penetrated these wildernesses. The very first, indeed, who wandered from the parent State over the Laurel Ridge, down into the unknown regions on its northwest, came avowedly as hunters and trappers; and such of them as escaped the tomahawk of the Indian, with very few exceptions, remained hunters and trappers till their deaths.

"But this first class of pioneers was not either numerous enough, or influential enough, to stamp its character upon the after-coming hundreds; and the second class of immigrants into Kentucky was composed of very different materials. Small farmers from North Carolina, Virginia, and Pennsylvania, for the most part, constituted this; and these daring adventurers brought with them intelligent and aspiring minds, industrious and persevering habits, a few of the comforts of civilized life, and some of the implements of husbandry. A number of them were men who had received the rudiments of an English education, and not a few of them had been reared up in the spirit, and a sincere observance of the forms, of religious worship. Many, perhaps most of them, were from the frontier settlements of the States named; and these combined the habits of the hunter and agriculturist, and possessed, with no inconsiderable knowledge of partially refined life, all that boldness and energy, which subsequently became so distinctive a trait of the character of the early settlers.

"This second class of the pioneers, or at least the mass of those who constituted it, sought the plains and forests, and streams of Kentucky, not to indulge any inclination for listless ramblings; nor as hunters or trappers; nor yet for the purpose of gratifying an awakened curiosity : they came deliberately, soberly, thoughtfully, *in search of a home,* determined, from the outset, to win one, or perish in the attempt; they came to cast their lot in a land that was new, to better their worldly condition by the acquisition of demesnes, to build up a new commonwealth in an unpeopled region; they came with their wives, and their children, and their kindred, from places where the toil of the hand,

and the sweat of the brow, could hardly supply them with bread, to a land in which ordinary industry would, almost at once, furnish all the necessaries of life, and where it was plain well-directed effort would ultimately secure its ease, its dignity, and its refinements. Poor in the past, and with scarce a hope, without a change of place, of a better condition of earthly ex-istence, either for themselves or their offspring, they saw themselves, *with* that change, rich in the future, and looked forward with cer-tainty to a time when their children, if not themselves, would be in a condition improved beyond compare.

" There was also a third class of pioneers, who in several respects differed as much from either the first or the second class, as these differed from each other. This class was composed, in great part, of men who came to Kentucky after the way had been in some measure prepared for immigrants, and yet before the setting in of that tide of population which, a year or two after the close of the American Revolution, poured so rapidly into these fertile regions from several of the Atlantic States. In this class of immigrants, there were many gentlemen of education, refinement, and no inconsiderable wealth: some of whom came to Kentucky as surveyors, others as commissioners from the parent State, and others again as land speculators; but most of them as *bona-fide* immigrants, determined to pitch their tents in the Great West, at once to become *units* of a new people, and to grow into affluence, and consideration, and renown, with the growth of a young and vigorous commonwealth.

"Such were the founders of Kentucky; and in them we behold the elements of a society inferior, in all the essentials of goodness and greatness, to none in the world. First came the hunter and trapper, to trace the river courses, and spy out the choice spots of the land; then came the small farmer and the hardy adventurer, to cultivate the rich plains discovered, and lay the nuclei of the towns and cities, which were so soon, and so rapidly, to spring up; and then came the surveyor, to mark the boundaries of individual possessions and give civil shape and

strength to the unformed mass, the speculator
to impart a new activity and keenness to the
minds of men, and the chivalrous and educated
gentleman, to infuse into the crude materials
here collected together the feelings and sentiments of refined existence, and to mould them
into forms of conventional beauty and social
excellence. Kentucky now began to have a
society, in which were the sinews of war, the
power of production, and the genius of improve
ment; and from this time, though still harassed,
as she had been from the beginning, by the inroads of a brave and determined enemy on her
north her advancement was regular and rapid."

CHAPTER VII.

Daniel Boone sets out for Kentucky with his family and his brother Squire Boone—Is joined by five families and forty men at Powell's Valley—The party is attacked by Indians and Daniel Boone's oldest son is killed—The party returns to the settlements on Clinch River—Boone, at the request of Governor Dunmore, goes to the West and conducts a party of surveyors to Virginia—Boone receives the command of three garrisons and the commission of captain—He takes a part in the Dunmore war—Battle of Point Pleasant and termination of the war.

HAVING completed all his arrangements for the journey, on the 25th of September, 1774, Daniel Boone, with his wife and children, set out on his journey to the West. He was accompanied by his brother, Squire Boone; and the party took with them cattle and swine with a view to the stocking of their farms, when they should arrive in Kentucky. Their bedding and other baggage was carried by pack-horses.

At a place called Powell's Valley, the party was reinforced by another body of emigrants to

the West consisting of five families and no less
than forty able-bodied men; well armed and
provided with provisions and ammunition.

They now went on in high spirits, "camping
out" every night in woods, under the shelter of
rude tents constructed with poles covered with
bed-clothes. They thus advanced on their
journey without accident or alarm, until the 6th
of October, when they were approaching a pass
in the mountains, called Cumberland Gap. The
young men who were engaged in driving the
cattle had fallen in rear of the main body a distance of five or six miles, when they were suddenly assailed by a party of Indians, who killed
six of their number and dispersed the cattle
in the woods. A seventh man escaped with a
wound. The reports of the musketry brought
the remainder of the party to the rescue, who
drove off the Indians and buried the dead.
Among the slain was the oldest son of Daniel
Boone.

A council was now held to determine on
their future proceedings. Notwithstanding the
dreadful domestic misfortune which he had ex-

perienced in the loss of his son, Daniel Boone
was for proceeding to Kentucky; in this opinion
he was sustained by his brother and some of the
other emigrants; but most of them were so
much disheartened by the misfortune they had
met with, that they insisted on returning; and
Boone and his brother yielding to their wishes,
returned to the settlement on the Clinch River
in the southwestern part of Virginia, a distance
of forty miles from the place where they had
been surprised by the Indians.

Here Boone was obliged to remain with his
family for the present; but he had by no means
relinquished his design of settling in Kentucky.
This delay, however, was undoubtedly a provi-
dential one; for in consequence of the murder
of the family of the Indian chief Logan, a terrible Indian war, called in history the Dunmore
War, was impending, which broke out in the
succeeding year, and extended to that part of
the West to which Boone and his party were
proceeding, when they were turned back by the
attack of the Indians.

In this war Daniel Boone was destined to

take an active part. In his autobiography, already quoted, he says:

"I remained with my family on Clinch until the 6th of June, 1774, when I and one Michael Stoner were solicited by Governor Dunmore, of Virginia, to go to the Falls of the Ohio, to conduct into the settlement a number of surveyors that had been sent thither by him some months before; this country having about this time drawn the attention of many adventurers. We immediately complied with the governor's request, and conducted in the surveyors, completing a tour of eight hundred miles, through many difficulties, in sixty-two days!

"Soon after I returned home, I was ordered to take command of three garrisons, during the campaign which Governor Dunmore carried on against the Shawanese Indians."

These three garrisons were on the frontier contiguous to each other; and with the command of them Boone received a commission as captain.

We quote from a contemporary an account of the leading events of this campaign, and of the battle of Point Pleasant, which may be said to have terminated the war. Whether Boone was present at this battle is uncertain; but his well-known character for ability and courage renders it probable that he took a part in the action.

"The settlers, now aware that a general warfare would be commenced by the Indians, immediately sent an express to Williamsburg, the seat of government in Virginia, communicating their apprehensions and soliciting protection.

"The Legislature was in session at the time, and it was immediately resolved upon to raise an army of about three thousand men, and march into the heart of the Indian country.

"One half of the requisite number of troops was ordered to be raised in Virginia, and marched under General Andrew Lewis across the country to the mouth of the Kanawha; and the remainder to be rendezvoused at Fort Pitt, and be commanded by Dunmore in person, who proposed to descend the Ohio and join Lewis at the place mentioned, from where the combined army was to march as circumstances might dictate at the time.

"By the 11th of September the troops under General Lewis, numbering about eleven hundred men, were in readiness to leave. The distance across to the mouth of the Kanawha, was near one hundred and sixty miles through an un-broken wilderness. A competent guide was secured, the baggage mounted on pack horses, and in nineteen days they arrived at the place of destination.

"The next morning after the arrival of the army at Point Pleasant, as the point of the land at the junction of the Kanawha and the Ohio was called, two men were out some distance from the camp, in pursuit of a deer, and were suddenly fired upon by a large body of Indians; one was killed, and the other with difficulty retreated back to the army, who hastily reported 'that he had seen a body of the enemy covering four acres of ground, as closely as they could stand by the side of each other.'

"General Lewis was a remarkably cool and considerate man; and upon being informed of this, 'after deliberately lighting his pipe,' gave orders that the regiment under his brother,

6

Colonel Charles Lewis, and another under Colo
nel Fleming, should march and reconnoiter the
enemy, while he would place the remainder of
the troops in order for battle. The two regiments marched without delay, and had not proceeded more than four hundred yards when
they were met by the Indians, approaching for
the same purpose. A skirmish immediately
ensued, and before the contest had continued
long, the colonels of the two regiments fell
mortally wounded, when a disorder in the ranks
followed, and the troops began a precipitate
retreat; but almost at this moment another regiment under Colonel Field arriving to their aid
and coming up with great firmness to the attack,
effectually checked the savages in the pursuit,
and obliged them in turn to give way till they
had retired behind a breastwork of logs and
brush which they had partially constructed.

"Lewis, on his arrival at the place, had encamped quite on the point of land between the
Ohio and Kanawha, and having moved but
a short distance out to the attack, the distance
across from river to river was still but short

The Indians soon extending their ranks entirely across, had the Virginians completely hemmed in, and in the event of getting the better of them, had them at their disposal, as there could have been no chance for escape.

"Never was ground maintained with more obstinacy; for it was slowly, and with no pre-cipitancy, that the Indians retired to their breastwork. The division under Lewis was first broken, although that under Fleming was nearly at the same moment attacked. This heroic officer first received two balls through his left wrist, but continued to exercise his com-mand with the greatest coolness and presence of mind. His voice was continually heard, 'Don't lose an inch of ground. Advance, out-flank the enemy, and get between them and the river.' But his men were about to be out-flanked by the body that had just defeated Lewis. Meanwhile the arrival of Colonel Field turned the fortune of the day, but not without a severe loss. Colonel Fleming was again wound-ed, by a shot through the lungs; yet he would not retire, and Colonel Field was killed as he

was leading on his men. The whole line of the
breastwork now became as a blaze of fire, which
lasted nearly till the close of the day. Here
the Indians under Logan, Cornstock, Elenipsico,
Red-Eagle, and other mighty chiefs of the tribes
of the Shawanese, Delawares, Mingos, Wyandots, and Cayugas, amounting, as was supposed,
to fifteen hundred warriors, fought, as men will
ever do for their country's wrongs, with a bravery which could only be equaled. The voice of
the great Cornstock was often heard during the
day, above the din of strife, calling on his men
in these words: 'Be strong ! Be strong !' And
when by the repeated charges of the whites,
some of his warriors began to waver, he is said
to have sunk his tomahawk into the head of one
who was basely endeavoring to desert. General
Lewis, finding at length that every charge upon
the lines of the Indians lessened the number of
his forces to an alarming degree, and rightly
judging that if the Indians were not routed before it was dark, a day of more doubt might
follow, he resolved to throw a body, if possible,
into their rear. As the good fortune of the

Virginians turned, the bank of the river favored this project, and forthwith three companies were detached upon the enterprise, under the three captains, Isaac Shelby (after renowned in the revolution, and since in the war with Canada), George Matthews, and John Stewart. These companies got unobserved to their place of destination upon Crooked Creek, which runs into the Kanawha. From the high weeds upon the bank of this little stream, they rushed upon the backs of the Indians with such fury, as to drive them from their works with precipitation. The day was now decided. The Indians, thus beset from a quarter they did not expect, were ready to conclude that a reinforcement had arrived. It was about sunset when they fled across the Ohio, and immediately took up their march for their towns on the Scioto."

Of the loss of both Indians and whites in this engagement, various statements have been given. A number amounting to seventy-five killed and one hundred and forty wounded of the whites has been rendered; with a loss on part of the

Indians not so great, but not correctly known.[*]
This was the severest battle ever fought with
the Indians in Virginia. Shortly after this
battle the Indians sent messengers to Governor
Dunmore, suing for peace, and a treaty was accordingly concluded. In this treaty the Indians
surrendered all claim to Kentucky. The Six
Nations had already done the same thing at the
Treaty of Fort Stanwix in 1768. The Cherokees had sold their claims to Henderson's company; so that when Boone settled in Kentucky
it was effectually cleared of all Indian titles.

[*] "History of the Backwoods."

CHAPTER VIII.

On the conclusion of Dunmore's war, the
militia were discharged from service, the garrisons which had been under Captain Daniel
Boone's command were broken up, and he once
more returned to his family, who were still
residing on Clinch River. But he was not long
permitted to remain comparatively idle. Captain Boone's character as an able officer and a
bold pioneer was now well known and appre-
ciated by the public. The marks of confidence

bestowed on him by Governor Dunmore rendered him one of the most conspicuous men in the Southern colonies, and his services were soon to be put in requisition by the most considerable and remarkable of all the parties of adventurers who ever sought a home in the West. This was Henderson's company, called the Transylvania Company, to whose proceedings we shall presently refer.

Between 1769 and 1773, various associations of men were formed, in Virginia and North Carolina, for visiting the newly-discovered regions and locating lands ; and several daring adventurers at different times during this period penetrated to the head-waters of the Licking River, and did some surveying ; but it was not till the year 1774 that the whites obtained any permanant foothold in Kentucky. From this year, therefore, properly dates the commencement of the early settlements of the State.*

The first great impetus given to adventure in Kentucky was by the bounty in Western lands given by Virginia to the officers and soldiers of

* Gallagher.

her own troops who had served in the British army in the old war in Canada between the English and French. These lands were to be surveyed on the Ohio River and its tributaries by the claimants thus created, who had the privilege of selecting them wherever they pleased within the prescribed regions. The first locations were made upon the Great Kanawha in the year 1772 and the next on the south side of the Ohio itself the following year. During this year likewise, extensive tracts of land were located on the north fork of the Licking, and surveys made of several salt licks, and other choice spots. But 1774 was more signalized than had been any preceding year by the arrival, in the new "land of promise," of the claimants to portions of its territory, and the execution of surveys. Among the hardy adventurers who descended the Ohio this year and penetrated to the interior of Kentucky by the river of that name, was James Harrod, who led a party of Virginians from the shores of the Monongahela. He disembarked at a point still known as "Harrod's Landing," and crossing the country

in a direction nearly west, paused in the midst of
a beautiful and fertile region, and *built the first
log-cabin* ever erected in Kentucky, on or near
the site of the present town of Harrodsburg.
This was in the spring, or early part of the summer, of 1774.*

The high-wrought descriptions of the country
northwest of the Laurel Ridge, which were
given by Daniel Boone upon his return to North
Carolina after his first long visit to Kentucky, cir-
culated with great rapidity throughout the entire
State, exciting the avarice of speculators and in
flaming the imaginations of nearly all classes of
people.   The organization of several companies,
for the purpose of pushing adventure in the new
regions and acquiring rights to land, was immediately attempted ; but that which commenced
under the auspices of Colonel Richard Henderson,
a gentleman of education and means, soon engaged public attention by the extent and boldness of its scheme, and the energy of its movements ; and either frightened from their purpose,
or attracted to its own ranks, the principal of

* Gallagher.

those individuals who had at first been active in endeavoring to form other associations.

The whole of that vast extent of country lying within the natural boundaries constituted by the Ohio, Kentucky, and Cumberland rivers, was at this time claimed by a portion of the Cherokee Indians, who resided within the limits of North Carolina ; and the scheme of Henderson's com- pany was nothing less than to take possession of this immense territory, under color of a purchase from those Indians, which they intended to make, and the preliminary negotiations for which were opened with the Cherokees, through the agency of Daniel Boone, as soon as the com- pany was fully organized. Boone's mission to the Indians having been attended with complete success, and the result thereof being conveyed to the company, Colonel Henderson at once started for Fort Wataga, on a branch of the Holston River, fully authorized to effect the purchase ; and here, on the 17th of March, 1775, he met the Indians in solemn council, delivered them a satisfactory consideration in merchandise, and received a deed signed by their head chiefs.

The purchase made, the next important step was to take possession of the territory thus acquired. The proprietors were not slow to do this, but immediately collected a small company of brave and hardy men, which they sent into Kentucky, under the direction of Daniel Boone, to open a road from the Holston to the Kentucky River, and erect a Station at the mouth of Otter Creek upon this latter.

After a laborious and hazardous march through the wilderness, during which four men were killed, and five others wounded, by trailing and skulking parties of hostile Indians, Boone and his company reached the banks of the Kentucky on the first of April, and descending this some fifteen miles, encamped upon the spot where Boonesborough now stands. Here the bushes were at once cut down, the ground leveled, the nearest trees felled, the foundations laid for a fort, and the first settlement of Kentucky commenced.

Perhaps the reader would like to see Boone's own account of these proceedings. Here is the passage where he mentions it in his autobiography. He has just been speaking of Governor Dunmore's war against the Shawanese Indians: "After the conclusion of which, he says, the militia was discharged from each garrison, and I being relieved from my post, was solicited by a number of North Carolina gentlemen, that were about purchasing the lands lying on the south side of Kentucky River from the Cherokee Indians, to attend their treaty at Wataga, in March, 1775, to negotiate with them, and mention the boundaries of the purchase. This I accepted; and at the request of the same gentlemen, undertook to mark out a road in the best passage through the wilderness to Kentucky with such assistance as I thought necessary to employ for such an important undertaking.

"I soon began this work, having collected a number of enterprising men, well armed. We proceeded with all possible expedition until we came within fifteen miles of where Boonesborough now stands, and where we were fired upon by a party of Indians, that killed two and wounded two of our number; yet, although surprised and taken at a disadvantage, we stood our ground. This was on the twentieth of March, 1775. Three days after we were fired upon again, and had two men killed and three wounded. Afterward we proceeded on to Kentucky River without opposition, and on the fifth day of April began to erect the fort of Boonesborough at a salt-lick, about sixty yards from the river, on the south side."

"On the fourth day, the Indians killed one of our men. We were busily engaged in building the fort, until the fourteenth day of June following, without any further opposition from the Indians."

In addition to this account by Captain Boone, we have another in a sort of official report made by him to Colonel Richard Henderson, the head of the company in whose service Boone was then employed. It is cited by Peck in his Life of Boone as follows:

April 15*th*, 1775.

"DEAR COLONEL: After my compliments to you, I shall acquaint you with our misfortune.

On March the 25th a party of Indians fired on
my company about half an hour before day, and
killed Mr. Twitty and his negro, and wounded
Mr. Walker very deeply; but I hope he will
recover.

"On March the 28th, as we were hunting for
provisions, we found Samuel Tate's son, who
gave us an account that the Indians fired on
their camp on the 27th day. My brother and
I went down and found two men killed and
scalped, Thomas McDowell and Jeremiah Mc-
Peters. I have sent a man down to all the
lower companies in order to gather them all to
the mouth of Otter Creek. My advice to you,
sir, is to come or send as soon as possible. Your
company is desired greatly, for the people are
very uneasy, but are willing to stay and venture
their lives with you, and now is the time to
frustrate their (the Indians,) intentions, and
keep the country whilst we are in it. If we
give way to them now, it will ever be the case,
This day we start from the battle-ground for
the mouth of Otter Creek, where we shall immediately erect a fort which will be done before

you can come or send; then we can send ten
men to meet you if you send for them.

"I am, sir, your most obedient,

"DANIEL BOONE.

"N. B.—We stood on the ground and guard-
ed our baggage till day, and lost nothing. We
have about fifteen miles to Cantuck at Otter
Creek."

Colonel Henderson was one of the most
remarkable men of his time. He was born in
Hanover County, Virginia, April 20th, 1735, the
same year with Boone. He studied law, and was
appointed judge of the Superior Court of North
Carolina under the Colonial Government. The
troubled times of the Regulators shut up the
courts of justice. In 1774 he engaged in his
grand scheme of founding the republic of Transylvania, and united with him John Williams,
Leonard Hendly Bullock, of Granville; William
Johnston, James Hogg, Thomas Hart, John
Luttrell, Nathaniel Hart, and David Hart, of
Orange County, in the company which made

the purchase of the immense tract of lands above referred to.

The company took possession of the lands on the 20th of April, 1775 ; the Indians appointing an agent to deliver them according to law.

The Governor of North Carolina, Martin, issued his proclamation in 1775, declaring this purchase illegal. The State subsequently granted 200,000 acres to the company in lieu of this.

The State of Virginia declared the same, but granted the company a remuneration of 200,000 acres, bounded by the Ohio and Green rivers. The State of Tennessee claimed the lands, but made a similar grant to the company in Powell's Valley. Thus, though the original scheme of founding an independent republic failed, the company made their fortunes by the speculation. Henderson died at his seat in Granville, January 30, 1785, universally beloved and respected.

What makes Henderson and his company particularly interesting to the admirers of Daniel Boone is, the strong probability that the purchase of the Cherokees was made on his representation and by his advice. This is the opinion of Judge Hall and of Mr. Peck, who also believe that Boone was already in the service of Henderson when he made his long journey to Kentucky. "This theory," says Mr. Peck, " explains why his brother, Squire Boone, came out with supplies, and why they examined the country so fully and particularly between the Kentucky and Cumberland rivers."

CHAPTER IX.

Description of the Old Fort at Boonesborough—Usual methods of fortification against the Indians—Arrival of more settlers at Boonesborough—Captain Boone returns to the Clinch River to bring out his family—He enlists new emigrants and starts for Kentucky—Reinforced by a large party at Powell's Valley—Arrival at Boonesborough—Arrival of many new settlers at Boonesborough and Harrod's settlement—Arrival of Kenton, Floyd, the McAfees, and other distinguished persons—Arrival of Colonel Richard Callaway.

As the old fort at Boonesborough became so celebrated in the Indian wars which followed its erection, our readers may be curious to know what sort of structure it was. We have accordingly copied from a print in Collins' Historical Sketches of Kentucky a view of the fort, from a drawing made by Colonel Henderson himself, and the following description: "It was situated adjacent to the river, with one of the angles resting on its bank near the water, and extending from it in the form of a parallelo

gram.   The length of the fort, allowing twenty
feet for each cabin and opening, must have been
about two hundred and sixty and the breadth
one hundred and fifty feet.   In a few days after
the work was commenced, one of the men was
killed by the Indians."   The houses, being built
of hewn logs, were bullet-proof.   They were of
a square form, and one of them projected from
each corner, being connected by stockades.   The
remaining space on the four sides, as will be
seen by the engraving, was filled up with cabins
erected of rough logs, placed close together.
The gates were on opposite sides, made of thick
slabs of timber, and hung on wooden hinges.
This was in accordance with the fashion of the
day.

  " A fort, in those rude military times," says
Butler,* "consisted of pieces of timber sharp-
ened at the end, and firmly lodged in the
ground: rows of these pickets enclosed the
desired space, which embraced the cabins of the
inhabitants. A block-house or more, of superior care and strength, commanding the sides

* History of Kentucky.

of the fort, with or without a ditch, completed
the fortifications or Stations, as they were called.
Generally the sides of the interior cabins formed
the sides of the fort. Slight as this advance
was in the art of war, it was more than sufficient against attacks of small arms in the hands
of such desultory warriors as their irregular
supply of provisions necessarily rendered the
Indians. Such was the nature of the military
structures of the provision against their enemies.
They were ever more formidable in the canebrakes and in the woods than before even these
imperfect fortifications."

We have seen in Boone's own account that
the fort at Boonesborough was completed on
the 14th of June, 1774. The buildings necessary for the accommodation and safety of the
little colony, and of the relatives and friends by
whom they expected to be joined during the
summer and fall, were completed about this
time. Colonel Henderson, Mr. John Luttrell,
and Mr. Nathaniel Hart, three of the proprietors, arrived at the station, which was now
named Boonesborough, in compliment to the

intrepid pioneer. These gentlemen brought
out with them between thirty and forty new
settlers, a goodly number of pack-horses, and
some of the necessaries of civilized life ; and the
Station, upon which various improvements were
soon made, at once became quite a bustling,
life-like, important *military* place. Much
pleased with the manner in which he had commenced the settlement of a new commonwealth,
and laid the foundations of what he doubted
not was soon to become a great city, Boone
took a part of his men and returned to the settlement on Clinch River, for the purpose of
setting an example to others by moving out his
own family.

The daring pioneer was now in high spirits,
and more than ever enraptured with the deep
forests and rich plains of Kentucky. He
sounded their praises without intermission
among the settlers on Clinch River, and soon
induced a number of persons to agree to accompany him on his return to Boonesborough. He
then went about making his domestic arrangements, for a final removal to Kentucky, with

great energy; and these being soon completed, in September or October he turned his back upon his old home forever, and started with his family and a few followers toward that which his unsurpassed daring and rude skill had prepared for them in a new land. In Powell's Valley he found Hugh McGary, Richard Hogan, and Thomas Denton, with their families and followers, awaiting his arrival. His companions, as now increased, amounted to twenty-six men, four women, and four or five boys and girls, perhaps half-grown; and placing himself at the head of this interesting little colony, he proudly led it through the Cumberland Gap into the wilderness beyond, where it was destined to be the germ of a great State.

When this party had arrived at the head of Dick's River, McGary, Denton, and Hogan, with their families and a few followers, separated themselves from the rest, and struck through the forest for the spot where Harrod and his Monongahelians had built their cabin the year before. Boone, with the main body of the party, continued his original course, and in due time

arrived safely at Boonesborough; "and Mrs.
Boone and her daughter," it is always recorded
with an air of pleasant exultation by the admirers
of the old pioneer, "were the earliest white
women in that region, and the first of their sex
and color that ever stood upon the banks of the
wild and beautiful Kentucky."

During the latter part of the year 1775, a
great many adventurers and surveyors, principally from Virginia and North Carolina, made
their appearance in Kentucky; and for all such
Boonesborough was a place of general rendezvous. Some united themselves to Boone's colony, and remained permanently at his Station:
others clustered around Harrod's Old Cabin,
and the Fort which had by this time been erected
by Logan, and made "improvements" in the
vicinity of each; but most of them returned to
their several homes after having made such
locations and surveys as they thought proper.
Among those by whom Boone was visited in
the course of this year were several men who
have subsequently rendered very important
services in the settlement of the West. and at

tained great and deserved celebrity: such were Simon Kenton, John Floyd, the four brothers McAfee, and others. A tolerably good road, sufficient for the passage of pack-horses in single file, had been opened from the settlements on the Holston to Boonesborough, by the party which Boone led out early in the following spring, and this now became the thoroughfare for other adventurers, a number of whom removed their families from North Carolina to Kentucky, and settled at Boonesborough, during the fall and winter of this year. Colonel Richard Callaway was one of these, and there were others of equal respectability.

CHAPTER X.

Disturbed state of the country in 1775—Breaking out of the Revolutionary war—Exposed situation of the Kentucky settlements—Hostility of the Indians excited by the British—First political convention in the West—Capture of Boone's daughter and the daughters of Colonel Callaway by the Indians—Their rescue by a party led by Boone and Callaway—Increased caution of the colonists at Boonesborough—Alarm and desertion of the Colonies in the West by land speculators and other adventurers—A reinforcement of forty-five men from North Carolina arrive at Boonesborough—Indian attack on Boonesborough in April—Another attack in July—Attack on Logan's Fort, and siege—Attack on Harrodsburg.

THE reader will not fail to remark that the period at which Daniel Boone commenced the settlement of Kentucky was the most eventful one in the history of our country. In the year 1775 hostilities between Great Britain and her American Colonies commenced at Lexington and Concord, and the whole country was mustering in arms at the time when Boone and the other Western emigrants were forming settlements four hundred miles beyond the frontier.

of Virginia and the Carolinas. Encouraged by the treaty of Lord Dunmore with the Indians in 1774, and knowing the Indian titles to the lands they were occupying to have been extinguished, they naturally counted on an unmolested possession of the region they were settling. But in this expectation they were sorely disappointed. The English officers and agents in the Northwest were indefatigable in stimulating the Indians to attack the American colonists in every quarter. They supplied them with arms and ammunition, bribed them with money, and aided and encouraged them to attack the feeble settlements in Kentucky and Tennessee. But Providence overruled these circumstances for the benefit of the Western country. "The settlement of Kentucky led to the conquest of the British posts in Illinois and Indiana, in 1778, and eventually threw the wide valleys of the West under control of the American Union." *

The settlers in Kentucky in 1775 were still acting under the belief that the claims purchased

* Peck. "Life of Daniel Boone."

by Henderson and Company from the Cherokees were valid, and that " the Proprietors of the Colony of Transylvania" were really founding a political State. Under this impression they took leases from the Company, and in the course of the year, eighteen delegates assembled in convention at Boonesborough, and acknowl-edged the Company as lawful proprietors, " es-tablished courts of justice, and rules for proceed-ing therein; also a militia law, a law for the preservation of game, and for appointing civil and militia officers." * This was the first po-litical convention ever held in the Western Valley for the formation of a free government.†

The winter and spring of 1776 ‡ were passed by the little colony of Boonesborough in hunt-ing, fishing, clearing the lands immediately con-tiguous to the station, and putting in a crop of corn. The colonists were molested but once by

* Butler. " History of Kentucky."
† Peck. " Life of Daniel Boone."
‡ Mr. Peck mentions the spring of 1776, as the date of the arrival at Boonesborough of Colonel Richard Callaway, and an intimate friend of Boone, with his family, and the family of Benjamin Logan, who had returned for them the preced ing autumn.

their enemies during the winter, when one man was killed by a small band of marauding Indians, who suddenly appeared in the vicinity, and as suddenly departed.

In the middle summer months, an incident of a thrilling character occurred, which cast a deep but only momentary shadow upon the little society of Boonesborough. This was the capture, by some skulking Indians belonging to a numerous band who were now prowling through the woods and brakes of Kentucky, and occasionally approaching the settlements for the purpose of plunder, of three young females, members of the families of Boone and Callaway.

This incident, which has been taken as the groundwork of two or three Western fictions, and also had thrown around it all the warm coloring of romance, by writers professing to deal only with the authentic, is thus briefly related in the papers of Colonel John Floyd, as quoted by Mr. Butler

" On the 7th of July, 1776, the Indians took out of a canoe which was in the river, within sight of Boonesborough, Miss Betsey Callaway, her sister Frances, and a daughter of Daniel Boone. The last two were about thirteen or fourteen years of age, and the other grown.

"The affair happened late in the afternoon, and the spoilers left the canoe on the opposite side of the river from us, which prevented our getting over for some time to pursue them. Next morning by daylight we were on the track, but found they had totally prevented our following them by walking some distance apart through the thickest cane they could find. We observed their course, however, and on which side they had left their sign, and traveled upward of thirty miles. We then imagined that they would be less cautious in traveling, and made a turn in order to cross their trace, and had gone but a few miles before we found their tracks in a buffalo-path.

"Pursuing this for the distance of about ten miles, we overtook them just as they were kindling a fire to cook. Our study had been more to get the prisoners without giving their captors time to murder them after they should discover us, than to kill the Indians.

" We discovered each other nearly at the same

time. Four of our party fired, and then all rushed upon them, which prevented their carrying anything away except one shot-gun without any ammunition. Mr. Boone and my-self had a pretty fair shot, just as they began to move off. I am well convinced I shot one through ; the one he shot dropped his gun, mine had none.

"The place was very thick with cane, and being so much elated on recovering the three little broken-hearted girls, prevented our mak-ing any further search. We sent them off without moccasins, and not one of them with so much as a knife or a tomahawk."

Although the people of the little colony of Boonesborough were not aware of the fact at the time, the marauding Indians who thus cap-tured Miss Boone and the Misses Callaway, as they were amusing themselves by paddling about the foot of the rock in the canoe, were one of the many scouting parties of Indians who were scattered about watching all the dif-ferent settlements in Kentucky, and preparing to attack them. The incident of the capture of the girls spread an alarm, and guards were stationed to defend the hands who were engaged in cultivating the ground.

Toward autumn the alarm of Indian hostilities, and the knowledge that war was raging throughout the Colonies east of the mountains, excited so much alarm, that some three hundred land speculators and other adventurers deserted the Western country and returned to their old homes.*

With the exception of the capture of the young girls mentioned above, no incident is recorded as having disturbed the tranquillity of Boonesborough during the year 1776. An occasional immigrant added a new member to its little society, who assisted in the labors of the hardy colonists on the surrounding grounds. But its numbers received no considerable increase till the following summer, when (25th July, 1777) a party of immigrants from North Carolina, consisting of forty-five men, arrived in the country, and took up their first abode in the wilderness at Boonesborough.

* Peck.

This was a fortunate circumstance for that station and great cause of rejoicing among all the settlements, for there were none of them that had not been much molested by the Indians since the opening of spring, and one or two of them had undergone long and regular Indian sieges.

Boonesborough had been surrounded by about one hundred of the enemy, as early as the middle of April, 1777, and fiercely attacked. But the Indians were so warmly received by the garrison on this occasion, that they in a very little time withdrew, having killed one of the settlers and wounded four others. Their own loss could not be ascertained.

Increased to two hundred warriors, this party had returned to the attack of Boonesborough on the fourth of July.* On the present occasion, having sent detachments to alarm and annoy the neighboring settlements, in order that no reinforcements should be sent to Boonesborough, the Indians encamped about the place, with the object of attempting its reduction by a regular

* Gallagher.

siege. After a close and vigorous attack for two days and nights, in which they succeeded in killing but one man and wounding four others the Indians, losing all hope of success, suddenly, and with great clamor, raised the siege, and disappeared in the adjacent forest. Their own loss was seven warriors, whose fall was noted from the fort.

After this attack, Boonesborough was disturbed no more by the Indians during the year. Had it been after the arrival of the immigrants above referred to, it would, in all probability, have taught its indefatigable enemies a lesson such as they had never then received at the hands of the Kentuckians.

But notwithstanding these two considerable attacks, and the " signs " of Indians in the surrounding forests for the whole summer, the men continued to clear the lands adjacent to the Station, and to cultivate corn and garden vegetables, some always keeping a vigilant look-out while the others labored. For supplies of meat they depended upon the forests, each of the men taking his turn as a hunter, at great hazard.

Meantime, the other settlements in Kentucky had suffered attacks from the Indians. Logan's Fort was invested by a force of one hundred Indians on the 20th of May, 1777, and after sustaining a vigorous siege for several days, was finally relieved by the timely arrival of a rein-forcement commanded by Colonel Bowman. On the 7th of March, 1777, the fort of Harrods-burg, then called Harrodstown, was assailed by a body of Indians, but they were speedily driven off, one of their number being killed. The whites had four men wounded, one of whom afterward died of his wounds.

CHAPTER XI.

Arrival of George Rogers Clark in Kentucky—Anecdote of his conversation with Ray—Clark and Jones chosen as delegates for the Colonies to the Virginia Legislature—Clark's important services in obtaining a political organization for Kentucky, and an abundant supply of gunpowder from the government of Virginia—Great labor and difficulty in bringing the powder to Harrodstown—Clark's expedition against Kaskaskias—Surprise and capture of their fort—Perilous and difficult march to Vincennes—Surprise and capture of that place—Extension of the Virginian settlements—Erection of Fort Jefferson.

Among the most celebrated pioneers of the West was General George Rogers Clark, who, at the time we are now writing of, bore the rank of Major. Anxious for the protection of the Western settlements, he was already planning his celebrated conquest of the British posts in the Northwest.

He first came to Kentucky in 1775 and penetrated to Harrodsburg, which had been reoccupied by Colonel Harrod. In this visit, from his well-known and commanding talents, he was voluntarily placed in command of the ir-

116

regular troops then in Kentucky. In the fall he returned to Virginia, and came back again to Kentucky in 1776. Mr. Butler relates the following anecdote, received from the lips of General Ray, as having occurred with General Clark upon his second visit: "I had come down," said General Ray, "to where I now live (about four miles north of Harrodsburg), to turn some horses in the range. I had killed a small blue-wing duck that was feeding in my spring, and had roasted it nicely on the brow of the hill, about twenty steps east of my house. After having taken it off to cool, I was much surprised on being suddenly accosted by a fine soldierly-looking man, who exclaimed, ' How do you do, my little fellow ? What is your name ? Ain't you afraid of being in the woods by your-self ?' On satisfying his inquiries, I invited the traveler to partake of my duck, which he did, without leaving me a bone to pick, his appetite was so keen, though he should have been welcome to all the game I could have killed, when I afterward became acquainted with his noble and gallant soul." After satisfying his questions, he inquired of the stranger his own name and business in this remote region. "My name is Clark," he answered, "and I have come out to see what you brave fellows are doing in Kentucky, and to lend you a helping hand if necessary." General Ray, then a boy of sixteen, conducted Clark to Harrodsburg, where he spent his time in observation on the condition and prospects of the country, natural to his comprehensive mind, and assisting at every opportunity in its defense.

At a general meeting of the settlers at Harrodstown, on the 6th of June, 1775, General George Rogers Clark and Gabriel John Jones were chosen to represent them in the Assembly of Virginia.

This, however, was not precisely the thing contemplated by Clark.* He wished that the people should appoint *agents*, with general powers to *negotiate* with the government of Virginia, and in the event that that commonwealth should refuse to recognize the colonists as within its jurisdiction and under its protec

* Collins.

tion, he proposed to employ the lands of the country as a fund to obtain settlers and establish an independent State. The election had, however, gone too far to change its object when Clark arrived at Harrodstown, and the gentlemen elected, although aware that the choice could give them no seat in the Legislature, proceeded to Williamsburg, at that time the seat of government. After suffering the most severe privations in their journey through the wilderness, the delegates found, on their arrival in Virginia, that the Legislature had adjourned, whereupon Jones directed his steps to the settlements on the Holston, and left Clark to attend to the Kentucky mission alone.

He immediately waited on Governor Henry, then lying sick at his residence in Hanover County, to whom he stated the objects of his journey. These meeting the approbation of the governor, he gave Clark a letter to the Executive Council of the State. With this letter in his hand he appeared before the Council, and after acquainting them fully with the condition and circumstances of the colony, he made application for five hundred-weight of gunpowder for the defense of the various stations. But with every disposition to assist and promote the growth of these remote and infant settlements, the Council felt itself restrained, by the uncertain and indefinite state of the relations existing between the colonists and the State of Virginia, from complying fully with his demand. The Kentuckians had not yet been recognized by the Legislature as citizens, and the proprietary claimants, Henderson & Co. were at this time exerting themselves to obtain from Virginia a relinquishment of her jurisdiction over the new territory. The Council, therefore, could only afford to *lend* the gunpowder to the colonists as *friends*, not *give* it to them as *fellow-citizens*.[*]

At the same time, they required Clark to be personally responsible for its value, in the event the Legislature should refuse to recognize the Kentuckians as citizens, and in the meantime to defray the expense of its conveyance to Kentucky. Upon these terms he did not feel at

* Collins.

liberty to accept the proffered assistance. He represented to the Council, that the emissaries of the British were employing every means to engage the Indians in the war; that the people in the remote and exposed Stations of Kentucky might be exterminated for the want of a supply which he, a private individual, had, at so much hazard and hardship, sought for their relief, and that, when this frontier bulwark was thus destroyed, the fury of the savages would burst like a tempest upon the heads of their own citizens.

To these representations, however, the Council remained inexorable; the sympathy for the frontier settlers was deep, but the assistance already offered was a stretch of power, and they could go no further. The keeper of the public magazine was directed to deliver the powder to Clark; but having long reflected on the situation, prospects, and resources of the new country, his resolution to reject the assistance, on the proposed conditions, was made before he left the Council chamber.

He determined to repair to Kentucky, as he had at first contemplated. to exert the resources of the country for the formation of an *Independent State*. He accordingly returned the order of the Council in a letter, setting forth his reasons for declining to accept their powder on these terms, and intimating his design of applying for assistance elsewhere, adding " that a country which was not worth defending was not worth claiming." On the receipt of this letter the Council recalled Clark to their presence, and an order was passed on the 23d of August, 1776, for the transmission of the gunpowder to Pitts-burg, to be there delivered to Clark, or his order, for the use of the people of Kentucky. This was the first act in that long and affectionate in-terchange of good offices which subsisted be-tween Kentucky and her parent State for so many years ; and obvious as the reflection is, it may not be omitted, that on the successful ter-mination of this negotiation hung the connection between Virginia and the splendid domain she afterward acquired west of the Alleghany Moun-tains.

At the fall session of the Legislature of Virginia, Messrs. Jones and Clark laid the Kentucky memorial before that body. They were, of course, not admitted to seats, though late in the session they obtained, in opposition to the exertions of Colonels Henderson and Campbell, the formation of the territory, which now comprises the present State of that name, into the County of Kentucky. The first efficient political organization of Kentucky was thus obtained through the sagacity, influence, and exertions of George Rogers Clark, who must be ranked as the earliest founder of that commonwealth. This act of the Virginia Legislature first gave it form and a political existence, and entitled it, under the constitution of Virginia, to a representation in the Assembly, as well as to a judicial and military establishment.

Having obtained these important advantages from their mission, they received the intelligence that the powder was still at Pittsburg, and they determined to take that point in their route home and carry it with them. The country around Pittsburg swarmed with Indians, evidently hostile to the whites, who would no doubt seek to interrupt their voyage.

These circumstances created a necessity for the utmost caution as well as expedition in their movements, and they accordingly hastily embarked on the Ohio with only seven boatmen. They were hotly pursued the whole way by Indians, but succeeded in keeping in advance until they arrived at the mouth of Limestone Creek, at the spot where the city of Maysville now stands. They ascended this creek a short distance with their boat, and concealed their cargo at different places in the woods along its banks. They then turned their boat adrift, and directed their course to Harrodstown, intending to return with a sufficient escort to insure the safe transportation of the powder to its destination. This in a short time was successfully effected, and the colonists were thus abundantly supplied with the means of defense against the fierce enemies who beset them on all sides.*

It was fortunate for Virginia, says a recent writer, † that she had at this time, on her western borders, an individual of rare military

---

* Collins. " Historical Sketches of Kentucky."
† Howe.   " Historical Collections of Virginia."

genius, in the person of Colonel George Rogers Clark, " *the Hannibal of the West*," who not only saved her back settlements from Indian fury, but planted her standard far beyond the Ohio. The Governor of the Canadian settlements in the Illinois country, by every possible method, instigated the Indians to annoy the frontier.

Virginia placed a small force of about 250 men under Clark, who, descending the Ohio, hid their boats, and marched northwardly, with their provisions on their backs. These being consumed, they subsisted for two days on roots, and, in a state of famine, appeared before Kaskaskias, unseen and unheard.

At midnight they surprised and took the town and fort, which had resisted a much larger force; then seizing the golden moment, sent a detachment who with equal success surprised three other towns. Rocheblave, the obnoxious Governor, was sent to Virginia. On his person were found written instructions from Quebec to excite the Indians to hostilities, and reward them for the scalps of the Americans.

The settlers transferred their allegiance to

Virginia, and she, as the territory belonged to her by conquest and charter, in the autumnal session of 1778 erected it into a county to be called Illinois. Insulated in the heart of the Indian country, in the midst of the most ferocious tribes, few men but Clark could have preserved this acquisition.

Hamilton, the Governor of Detroit, a bold and tyrannical personage, determined, with an overwhelming force of British and Indians, to penetrate up the Ohio to Fort Pitt, to sweep all the principal settlements in his way, and besiege Kaskaskias. Clark despaired of keeping possession of the country, but he resolved to preserve this post, or die in its defense. While he was strengthening the fortifications, he received information that Hamilton, who was at Fort St. Vincent (Vincennes), had weakened his force by sending some Indians against the frontiers.

This information, to the genius of Clark, disclosed, with the rapidity of an electric flash, not only safety but new glory. To resolve to attack Hamilton before he could collect the Indians was the work of a moment—the only hope of saving the country. With a band of 150 gallant and hardy comrades, he marched across the country. It was in February, 1779. When within nine miles of the enemy, it took these intrepid men five days to cross the drowned lands of the Wabash, having often to wade up to their breasts in water. Had not the weather been remarkably mild, they must have perished.

On the evening of the 23d, they landed in sight of the fort, before the enemy knew any-thing of their approach. After a siege of eigh-teen hours it surrendered, without the loss of a man to the besiegers. The Governor was sent prisoner to Williamsburg, and considerable stores fell into the possession of the conqueror.

Other auspicious circumstances crowned this result. Clark, intercepting a convoy from Canada, on their way to this post, took the mail, forty prisoners, and goods to the value of $45,000; and to crown all, his express from Vir-ginia arrived with the thanks of the Assembly to him and his gallant band for their reduction of the country about Kaskaskias. This year

Virginia extended her western establishments through the agency of Colonel Clark, and had several fortifications erected, among which was Fort Jefferson, on the Mississppi. *

* Howe.

CHAPTER XII.

Scarcity of salt at Boonesborough—Boone goes to Blue Licks to make salt, and is captured by the Indians—Taken to Chillicothe—Affects contentment, and deceives the Indians —Taken to Detroit—Kindness of the British officers to him —Returns to Chillicothe—Adopted into an Indian family— Ceremonies of adoption—Boone sees a large force of Indians destined to attack Boonesborough—Escapes, and gives the alarm, and strengthens the fortifications at Boonesborough —News of delay by the Indians on account of Boone's escape—Boone goes on an expedition to the Scioto—Has a fight with a party of Indians—Returns to Boonesborough, which is immediately besieged by Captain Duquesne with five hundred Indians—Summons to surrender—Time gained —Attack commenced—Brave defense—Mines and counter-mines—Siege raised—Boone brings his family once more back to Boonesborough, and resumes farming.

WHILE George Rogers Clark was engaged in his campaign against the British posts in the Northwest, Daniel Boone was a prisoner among the Indians. The people at Boonesborough were suffering for want of salt. It could not be obtained conveniently from the Atlantic Colonies, but it could be manufactured at a place called the Blue Licks, from salt water which abounded there.

9

In January, 1778, accompanied by thirty men,
Boone went to the Blue Licks to make salt for
the different Stations; and on the 7th of February following, while out hunting, he fell in
with one hundred and two Indian warriors, on
their march to attack Boonesborough. He instantly fled, but being upward of fifty years
old, he was unable to outstrip the fleet young
men who pursued him, and was a second time
taken prisoner. As usual, he was treated with
kindness until his final fate should be determined, and was led back to the Licks, where
his party were still encamped. Here Boone
surrendered his whole party to the number of
twenty-seven, upon a promise on the part of
the Indians of life and good treatment, both
of which conditions were faithfully observed.
This step was apparently unnecessary; but the
result showed that it was a master stroke of
policy on Boone's part. He knew the nature of
the Indians, and foresaw that they would forthwith return home with their prisoners, and thus
save Boonesborough from attack.

Had the Indians gone on to that place, by

snowing their prisoners and threatening to put them to the torture, they might have obtained important results. But they did nothing of the kind. As Boone had calculated, they went home with their prisoners and booty.

Captain Boone has been censured for the surrender of his men, which he made at his own capture, and at a subsequent period was tried by court-martial and acquitted. This was a just decision. The surrender caused the Indians to return home with their prisoners instead of attacking Boonesborough, which would almost certainly have been taken and destroyed if this surrender had not been made.

Elated with their unexpected success, the Indians now returned at once to old Chillicothe, the principal town of the Shawnees, on the Little Miami, treating their prisoners, during a march of three days in very cold and inclement weather, as well as they fared themselves, as regarded fire and provisions. Boone and his companions were kept in captivity by the Indians, and closely watched for several weeks, when the old pioneer and ten of his men were con ducted to Detroit, then a British garrison, and all but Boone presented to the commandant, by whom they were all well treated. For the old pioneer himself, the Indians had conceived a particular liking; and they stubbornly refused to give him up, though several gentlemen of Detroit were very anxious they should leave him, and the commandant offered to ransom him by a liberal sum. He was therefore compelled to accompany them back to Chillicothe, their town on the Little Miami; which they reached after a march of fifteen days.

Boone was now formally adopted as a son in one of the Indian families. "The forms of the ceremony of adoption," says Mr. Peck,* " were often severe and ludicrous. The hair of the head is plucked out by a painful and tedious operation, leaving a tuft, some three or four inches in diameter, on the crown for the scalp-lock, which is cut and dressed up with ribbons and feathers. The candidate is then taken into the river in a state of nudity, and there thoroughly washed and rubbed, 'to take all his

* "Life of Daniel Boone."

white blood out.' This ablution is usually performed by females. He is then taken to the
council-house, where the chief makes a speech,
in which he expatiates upon the distinguished
honors conferred on him. His head and face
are painted in the most approved and fashionable style, and the ceremony is concluded with
a grand feast and smoking."

After undergoing after this fashion what was
not inaptly termed the Indian toilet, Boone
was considered a regular member of the tribe,
and by judiciously accommodating himself to
his new condition, he rapidly won upon the
regards of the Indians, and soon secured their
confidence. They challenged him to a trial of
skill at their shooting-matches—in which he took
care not to excel them—invited him to accompany them on their hunting excursions, bestowed particular notice upon him in various ways,
and always treated him with much consideration. As regarded merely his physical comfort, Boone's situation was, at this time, rather
enviable than otherwise ; but he felt a depressing anxiety with regard to his wife and chil-

dren, and doubted the safety and prosperity of
the Station, without his own watchfulness and
superintendence. He therefore determined to
escape from his captors at the earliest possible
period, and very impatiently waited an opportunity for accomplishing this purpose.

Early in June a party of Indians went to the
Scioto Licks to make salt. Boone was taken
with them, but kept so constantly employed at
the kettles, that he found no chance of escaping.
Having sufficiently supplied themselves with
the desired article, the party returned; and at
the Chillicothe town Boone found four hundred
and fifty Indian warriors, armed well and painted
in a most frightful manner, ready to march
against Boonesborough: this was on the fifteenth
or sixteenth of the month.

Boone now saw the absolute necessity of escaping at once, and determined to make the
attempt without delay. He rose at the usual
time the next morning, and went out upon
a hunt. His object was to give his wary
masters the slip, in such a manner as would be
least likely to excite their suspicions, and be

the longest in determining them upon a pursuit.

No sooner was he at such a distance from the town as would prevent observations of his movements, than he struck out rapidly in the direction of Boonesborough. So great was his anxiety, that he stopped not to kill anything to eat, but performed his journey—a distance of one hundred and sixty miles—in less than five days, upon one meal, which, before starting, he had concealed in his basket. On arriving at Boonesborough, he found the fort, as he feared he should, in a bad state for defense; but his activity soon strengthened it, and his courage at once reinspired the sinking hearts of the garrison. Everything was immediately put in proper condition for a vigorous defense, and all became impatient for intelligence of the movements of the enemy.

A few days after Boone's escape from the Indians, one of his fellow-prisoners succeeded likewise in eluding their vigilance, and made his way safely and expeditiously to Boonesborough. This man arrived at the Station at a time when the garrison were hourly expecting the appearance of the enemy, and reported that, on account of Boone's elopement, the Indians had postponed their meditated invasion of the settled regions for three weeks.* It was discovered, however, that they had their spies in the country, watching the movements of the different garrisons; and this rendered the settlers wary and active, and gave all the Stations time and opportunity to strengthen themselves, and make every preparation for a powerful resistance of what, they could not but believe, was to be a long and great effort to drive them from the land, and utterly destroy their habitations.

Week passed after week, but no enemy appeared. The state of anxiety and watchfulness in which the garrison at Boonesborough had, for so long a time, been kept, was becoming irksome, and the men were beginning to relax in their vigilance. This Boone observed, and it determined him to undertake an expedition, which he had been probably meditating for

* Gallagher.

some time. On the 1st of August, therefore, with a company of nineteen of the brave spirits by whom he was surrounded, he left the fort with the intention of marching against and surprising one of the Indian towns on the Scioto. He advanced rapidly, but with great caution, and had reached a point within four or five miles of the town destined to taste of his vengeance, when he met its warriors, thirty in number, on their way to join the main Indian force, then on its march toward Boonesborough.

An action immediately commenced, which terminated in the flight of the Indians, who lost one man and had two others wounded.

Boone received no injury, but took three horses, and all the "plunder" of the war party. He then despatched two spies to the Indian town, who returned with the intelligence that it was evacuated. On the receipt of this information, he started for Boonesborough with all possible haste, hoping to reach the Station before the enemy, that he might give warning of their approach, and strengthen its numbers. He passed the main body of the Indians on the sixth day of his march, and on the seventh reached Boonesborough.

On the eighth day the enemy's force marched up, with British colors flying, and invested the place. The Indian army was commanded by Captain Duquesne, with eleven other Canadian Frenchmen and several distinguished chiefs, and was the most formidable force which had yet invaded the settlements. The commander summoned the garrison to surrender in the name of his Britannic Majesty.

Boone and his men, perilous as was their situation, received the summons without apparent alarm, and requested a couple of days for the consideration of what should be done. This was granted; and Boone summoned his brave companions to council: *but fifty men appeared!* Yet these fifty, after a due consideration of the terms of capitulation proposed, and with the knowledge that they were surrounded by savage and remorseless enemies to the number of about *five hundred*, determined, unanimously, to "*defend the fort as long as a man of them lived!*"

The two days having expired, Boone announced this determination from one of the bastions, and thanked the British commander for the notice given of his intended attack, and the time allowed the garrison for preparing to defend the Station. This reply to his summons was entirely unexpected by Duquesne, and he heard it with evident disappointment. Other terms were immediately proposed by him, which "sounded so gratefully in the ears" of the garrison that Boone agreed to treat; and, with eight of his companions, left the fort for this purpose. It was soon manifest, however, by the conduct of the Indians, that a snare had been laid for them; and escaping from their wily foes by a sudden effort, they re-entered the palisades, closed the gates, and betook themselves to the bastions.

A hot attack upon the fort now instantly commenced but the fire of the Indians was returned from the garrison with such unexpected briskness and fatal precision that the besiegers were compelled to fall back. They then sheltered themselves behind the nearest trees and

stumps and continued the attack with more
caution. Losing a number of men himself, and
perceiving no falling off in the strength or
the marksmanship of the garrison, Duquesne
resorted to an expedient which promised greater
success.

The fort stood upon the bank of the river,
about sixty yards from its margin; and the
purpose of the commander of the Indians was
to undermine this, and blow up the garrison.
Duquesne was pushing the mine under the fort
with energy when his operations were discovered
by the besieged. The miners precipitated the
earth which they excavated into the river; and
Boone, perceiving that the water was muddy
below the fort, while it was clear above, instantly divined the cause, and at once ordered
a deep trench to be cut inside the fort, to coun-
teract the work of the enemy.

As the earth was dug up, it was thrown over
the wall of the fort, in the face of the besieging
commander. Duquesne was thus informed that
his design had been discovered; and being convinced of the futility of any further attempts

of that kind he discontinued his mining operations, and once more renewed the attack upon the
Station in the manner of a regular Indian siege.
His success, however, was no better than it had
been before; the loss appeared to be all upon
his side; his stock of provisions was nearly ex·
hausted; having for nine days tried the bravery
of his savage force, and tasked his own in·
genuity to its utmost, he raised the siege, and
abandoned the grand object of the expedi·
tion.

During this siege, " the most formidable," says
Mr. Marshall, "that had ever taken place in
Kentucky from the number of Indians, the skill
of the commanders, and the fierce countenances
and savage dispositions of the warriors," only
two men belonging to the Station were killed,
and four others wounded.

Duquesne lost thirty-seven men, and had
many wounded, who, according to the invariable
usage of the Indians, were immediately borne
from the scene of action.

Boonesborough was never again disturbed by
any formidable body of Indians. New Stations

were springing up every year between it and
the Ohio River, and to pass beyond these
for the purpose of striking a blow at an older
and stronger enemy, was a piece of folly of
which the Indians were never known to be
guilty.

During Boone's captivity among the Shawnees, his family, supposing that he had been
killed, had left the Station and returned to their
relatives and friends in North Carolina; and as
early in the autumn as he could well leave, the
brave and hardy warrior started to move them
out again to Kentucky. He returned to the
settlement with them early the next summer,
and set a good example to his companions by
industriously cultivating his farm, and volun-
teering his assistance, whenever it seemed needed,
to the many immigrants who were now pouring
into the country, and erecting new Stations in
the neighborhood of Boonesborough. He was
a good as well as a great man in his sphere,
says Mr. Gallagher (our chief authority for the
foregoing incidents); and for his many and important services in the early settlements of Ken-

tucky, he well deserved the title of Patriarch which was bestowed upon him during his life, and all the praises that have been sung to his memory since his death.*

* W. D. Gallagher, in " Hesperian."

CHAPTER XIII.

Captain Boone tried by court-martial—Honorably acquitted and promoted—Loses a large sum of money—His losses by lawsuits and disputes about land—Defeat of Colonel Rogers's party—Colonel Bowman's expedition to Chillicothe—Arrival near the town—Colonel Logan attacks the town—Ordered by Colonel Bowman to retreat—Failure of the expedition—Consequences to Bowman and to Logan.

SOME complaint having been made respecting Captain Boone's surrender of his party at the Blue Licks, and other parts of his military conduct, his friends, Colonel Richard Callaway and Colonel Benjamin Logan, exhibited charges against him which occasioned his being tried by court-martial. This was undoubtedly done with a view to put an end to the calumny by disproving or explaining the charges. The result of the trial was an honorable acquittal, increased popularity of the Captain among his fellow-citizens, and his promotion to the rank of Major.*

* Peck.

144

While Boone had been a prisoner among the Indians, his wife and family, supposing him to be dead, had returned to North Carolina. In the autumn of 1778 he went after them to the house of Mrs. Boone's father on the Yadkin.

In 1779, a commission having been opened by the Virginia Legislature to settle Kentucky land claims, Major Boone " laid out the chief of his little property to procure land warrants, and having raised about twenty thousand dollars in paper money, with which he intended to pur- chase them, on his way from Kentucky to Rich- mond, he was robbed of the whole, and left destitute of the means of procuring more. This heavy misfortune did not fall on himself alone. Large sums had been intrusted to him by his friends for similar purposes, and the loss was extensively felt."

Boone must have suffered much anxiety in consequence of this affiair. Little is known re- specting it, excepting that it did not impair the confidence of his friends in his perfect integrity.

This appears in the following extract of a letter from Colonel Thomas Hart, late of Lexington, Kentucky, to Captain Nathaniel Hart, dated Grayfields, August 3d, 1780.

" I observe what you say respecting our losses by Daniel Boone. [Boone had been robbed of funds in part belonging to T. and N. Hart.] I had heard of the misfortune soon after it happened, but not of my being partaker before now. I feel for the poor people, who, perhaps, are to lose even their pre-emptions : but I must say, I feel more for Boone, whose character, I am told, suffers by it. Much degenerated must the people of this age be, when amongst them are to be found men to censure and blast the reputation of a person so just and upright, and in whose breast is a seat of virtue too pure to admit of a thought so base and dishonorable. I have known Boone in times of old, when poverty and distress had him fast by the hand; and in these wretched circumstances, I have ever found him of a noble and generous soul, despising everything mean ; and therefore I will freely grant him a discharge for whatever sums of mine he might have been possessed of at the time."

Boone's ignorance of legal proceedings, and

his aversion to lawsuits, appear to have occasioned the loss of his real estate ; and the loose manner in which titles were granted, one conflicting with another, occasioned similar losses to much more experienced and careful men at the same period.

During the year 1779 the emigration to Kentucky was much greater than any previous one. The settlers do not seem to have been so much annoyed by the Indians as formerly. Yet this year is distinguished in the annals of Kentucky for the most bloody battle ever fought between the whites and Indians within her borders, with the single exception of that of the Blue Licks.

It took place opposite to Cincinnati. Colonel Rogers had been down to New Orleans to procure supplies for the posts on the Upper Mississippi and Ohio. Having obtained them, he ascended these rivers until he reached the place mentioned above. Here he found the Indians in their canoes coming out of the mouth of the Little Miami, and crossing to the Kentucky side of the Ohio. He conceived the plan of surprising them as they landed. The Ohio was

very low on the Kentucky side, so that a large
sand-bar was laid bare, extending along the
shore.   Upon this Rogers landed his men, but,
before they could reach the spot where they expected to attack the enemy they were themselves attacked by such superior numbers that
the issue of the contest was not doubtful for a
single moment.   Rogers and the greater part of
his men were instantly killed.   The few who
were left fled toward the boats.   But one of
them was already in the possession of the Indians, whose flanks were extended in advance of
the fugitives, and the few men remaining in the
other pushed off from shore without waiting to
take their comrades on board.   These last now
turned around upon their pursuers, and, furiously
charging them, a small number broke through
their ranks and escaped to Harrodsburg.   The
loss in this most lamentable affair was about sixty
men, very nearly equal to that at Blue Licks.

The Kentuckians resolved to invade the Indian country, and Chillicothe was selected as
the point to feel the weight of their vengeance.
Colonel Bowman issued a call, inviting all those

who were willing to accompany him in the expedition to rendezvous at Harrodsburg. This was the manner of organizing such expeditions in Kentucky. An officer would invite volunteers to participate with him in an incursion into the Indian country. All who joined were expected to submit to his direction.

On this occasion there was no want of zeal among the people. Bowman's reputation as a soldier was good, and three hundred men were soon collected, among whom were Logan and Harrod, both holding the rank of captain. It does not appear that either Boone or Kenton engaged in this enterprise. Indeed, the first is said to have been absent in North Carolina, his family having returned there after his capture in the preceding year, supposing him to be dead.

The expedition moved in the month of July—its destination well known—and its march so well conducted that it approached its object without discovery. From this circumstance, it would seem that the Indians were but little apprehensive of an invasion from those who had never before ventured on it, and whom they were in

the habit of invading annually; or else so secure
in their own courage that they feared no enemy,
for no suspecting spy was out to foresee approaching danger. Arrived within a short distance of
the town, night approached, and Colonel Bow
man halted. Here it was determined to invest
and attack the place just before the ensuing day,
and several dispositions were then made very
proper for the occasion, indicating a considerable
share of military skill and caution, which gave
reasonable promise of a successful issue. At a
proper hour the little army separated, after a
movement that placed it near the town, the one
part, under the command of Bowman in person
—the other, under Captain Logan; to whom
precise orders had been given to march, on the
one hand, half round the town; while the Colonel, passing the other way, was to meet him,
and give the signal for an assault. Logan immediately executed his orders, and the place was
half enveloped. But he neither saw nor heard
the commander-in-chief. Logan now ordered
his men to conceal themselves in the grass and
weeds, and behind such other objects as were

present, as the day began to show itself, and he had not yet received the expected order to begin the attack; nor had he been able, though anxious, to ascertain what had intercepted or delayed his superior officer. The men, on shifting about for hiding-places, had alarmed one of the Indians' dogs, who forthwith set to barking with the agitation of apparent fright. This brought out an Indian warrior, who proceeded with caution on the way that the dog seemed to direct his own attention, and in a short time, if he had continued his progress, might have been made a prisoner; but, at this critical moment, one of the party with the Colonel fired his gun; which the Indian, well understanding as coming from an enemy, gave an instantaneous and loud whoop, and ran immediately to his cabin. The alarm was instantly spread through the town, and preparation made for defense. The party with Logan was near enough to hear the bustle and to see the women and children escaping to the cover of the woods by a ridge which ran between them and where Colonel Bowman with his men had halted.

In the meantime the warriors equipped themselves with their military habiliments, and repaired to a strong cabin; no doubt, designated
in their councils for the like occurrences. By
this time daylight had disclosed the whole scene,
and several shots were discharged on the one
side, and returned from the other, while some
of Logan's men took possession of a few cabins,
from which the Indians had retreated—or rather
perhaps it should be said, repaired to their
stronghold, the more effectually to defend themselves. The scheme was formed by Logan, and
adopted by his men in the cabins, of making a
movable breastwork out of the doors and floor—
and of pushing it forward as a battery against
the cabin in which the Indians had taken post;
others of them had taken shelter from the fire of
the enemy behind stumps, or logs, or the vacant
cabins, and were waiting orders; when the
Colonel finding that the Indians were on their
defense, despatched orders for a retreat. This
order, received with astonishment, was obeyed
with reluctance; and what rendered it the more
distressing, was the unavoidable exposure which

the men must encounter in the open field, or prairie, which surrounded the town: for they were apprised that from the moment they left their cover, the Indians would fire on them, until they were beyond the reach of their balls. A retreat, however, was deemed necessary, and every man was to shift for himself. Then, instead of one that was orderly, commanding, or supported—a scene of disorder, unmilitary and mortifying, took place; here a little squad would rush out of or break from behind a cabin—there individuals would rise from a log, or start up from a stump, and run with all speed to gain the neighboring wood.

At length, after the loss of several lives, the remnant of the invading force was reunited, and the retreat continued in tolerable order, under the painful reflection that the expedition had failed, without any adequate cause being known. This was, however, but the introduction to disgrace, if not of misfortune still more extraordinary and distressing. The Indian warriors, commanded by Blackfish, sallied from the town, and commenced a pursuit of the discomfited in

vaders of their forests and firesides, which they
continued for some miles, harassing and galling
the rear of the fugitives without being checked,
notwithstanding the disparity of numbers,
there not being more than thirty of the savages
in pursuit. Bowman, finding himself thus
pressed, at length halted his men in a low piece
of ground covered with brush; as if he sought
shelter from the enemy behind or among them.
A situation more injudiciously chosen, if chosen
at all, cannot be easily imagined—since of all
others it most favored the purposes of the
Indians. In other respects the commander
seems also to have lost his understanding—he
gave no orders to fire—made no detachment to
repulse the enemy, who, in a few minutes, by
the whoops, yells, and firing, were heard on all
sides—but stood as a mark to be shot at or one
panic-struck. Some of the men fired, but without any precise object, for the Indians were
scattered and hid by the grass and bushes.
What would have been the final result it is difficult to conjecture, if Logan, Harrod, Bulger,
and a few others had not mounted some of the

pack-horses and scoured the woods, first in one direction, then in another; rushing on the Indians wherever they could find them, until very fortunately Blackfish was killed; and this being soon known, the rest fled. It was in the evening when this event occurred, which being reported to the Colonel, he resumed his march at dark—taking for his guide a creek near at hand, which he pursued all night without any remarkable occurrence—and in quiet and safety thence returned home, with the loss of nine men killed and another wounded: having taken two Indian scalps: which, however, was thought a trophy of small renown.

A somewhat different account is given by some, in which Bowman is exculpated from all blame. According to this, it was the vigorous defense of the Indians which prevented him from fulfilling his part of the combinations. Be this as it may, it is certain that Bowman lost reputation by the expedition; while, on the other hand the conduct of Logan raised him still higher in the estimation of the people.

CHAPTER XIV.

THE year 1780 was distinguished for two events of much importance: the invasion of Kentucky by the British and Indians, under Colonel Byrd, and General Clark's attack upon the Shawanee towns. The first of these was a severe and unexpected blow to Kentucky. Marshall says that the people in their eagerness to take up land had almost forgotten the existence of hostilities. Fatal security, and most fatal with such a foe, whose enterprises were

156

conducted with such secrecy that their first announcement was their presence in the midst of the unprepared settlement. In fact, the care lessness of the Western borderers is often unaccountable, and this is not the least surprising instance of it.

That they did not anticipate an attempt to retaliate the incursion of Bowman into the Indian country is indeed astonishing. It was very fortunate for the Kentuckians that their enemies were as little gifted with perseverance as they were with vigilance. This remark is to be understood in a restricted sense of both parties. When once aroused to a sense of their danger none were more readily prepared, or more watchful to meet it than the settlers; and on the other hand, nothing could exceed the perseverance of the Indians in the beginning of their enterprises, but on the slightest success (not reverse) they wished to return to exhibit their trophies at home. Thus, on capturing Boone and his party, instead of pushing on and attacking the settlements which were thus weakened, they returned to display their prisoners.

The consequences were that these defects neutralized each other, and no very decisive strokes were made by either side. But the English Governor Hamilton, who had hitherto contented himself with stimulating the Indians to hostilities, now aroused by the daring and success of Clark, prepared to send a powerful expedition by way of retaliation, against the settlements. Colonel Byrd was selected to command the forces, which amounted to six hundred men, Canadians and Indians. To render them irresistible, they were supplied with two pieces of artillery. The posts on the Licking were the first objects of the expedition.

In June they made their appearance before Ruddle's Station; and this, it is said, was the first intimation that the garrison had received of their danger, though Butler states that the enemy were twelve days on their march from the Ohio. The incidents of the invasion are few. The fort at Ruddle's Station was in no condition to resist so powerful an enemy backed by artillery, the defenses being nowise superior to those we have before described.

They were summoned to surrender in the name of his Britannic Majesty, with the promise of protection for their lives only. What could they do? The idea of resisting such a force was vain. The question presented itself to them thus: Whether they should surrender at once and give up their property, or enrage the Indians by a fruitless resistance, and lose their property and lives also. The decision was quickly made, the post was surrendered and the enemy thronged in, eager for plunder. The inmates of the fort were instantly seized, families were separated; for each Indian caught the first person whom he met, and claimed him or her as his prisoner. Three who made some resistance were killed upon the spot. It was in vain that the settlers remonstrated with the British commander. He said it was impossible to restrain them. This doubtless was true enough, but he should have thought of it before he assumed the command of such a horde, and consented to lead them against weak settlements.

The Indians demanded to be led at once against Martin's Fort, a post about five miles distant. Some say that the same scene was enacted over here; but another account states that so strongly was Colonel Byrd affected by the barbarities of the Indians, that he refused to advance further, unless they would consent to allow him to take charge of all the prisoners who should be taken. The same account goes on to say that the demand was complied with, and that on the surrender of Martin's Fort, this arrangement was actually made; the Indians taking possession of the property and the British of the prisoners. However this may be, the capture of this last-mentioned place, which was surrendered under the same circumstances as Ruddle's, was the last operation of that campaign. Some quote this as an instance of weakness; Butler, in particular, contrasts it with the energy of Clark.

The sudden retreat of the enemy inspired the people with joy as great as their consternation had been at the news of his unexpected advance. Had he pressed on, there is but little doubt that all the Stations would have fallen into his hands, for there were not men enough to spare from them to meet him in the field. The greatest difficulty would have been the carriage of the artillery. The unfortunate people who had fallen into the hands of the Indians at Ruddle's Station were obliged to accompany their captors on their rapid retreat, heavily laden with the plunder of their own dwellings. Some returned after peace was made, but too many, sinking under the fatigues of the journey, perished by the tomahawk.

Soon after the retreat of the enemy, General Clark, who was stationed at Fort Jefferson, called upon the Kentuckians to join him in an invasion of the Indian country. The reputation of Clark caused the call to be responded to with great readiness. A thousand men were collected, with whom Clark entered and devastated the enemy's territory. The principal towns were burned and the fields laid waste. But one skir-mish was fought, and that at the Indian village of Pickaway. The loss was the same on both sides, seventeen men being killed in each army. Some writers who have not the slightest objec-tion to war very gravely express doubts as to whether the expedient of destroying the crops of the Indians was justifiable. It is generally treated by these men as if it was a wanton display of a vindictive spirit, when in reality it was dictated by the soundest policy; for when the Indians' harvests were destroyed, they were compelled to subsist their families altogether by hunting and had no leisure for their murderous inroads upon the settlements. This result was plainly seen on this occasion, for it does not appear that the Indians attacked any of the settlements during the remainder of this year.

An adventure which occurred in the spring, but was passed over for the more important operations of the campaign, claims our attention, presenting as it does a picture of the varieties of this mode of warfare. We quote from McClung:

"Early in the spring of 1780 Mr. Alexander McConnell, of Lexington, Kentucky, went into the woods on foot to hunt deer. He soon killed a large buck, and returned home for a horse in order to bring it in. During his absence a party of five Indians, on one of their

usual skulking expeditions, accidentally stum
bled on the body of the deer, and perceiving
that it had been recently killed, they naturally
supposed that the hunter would speedily return
to secure the flesh. Three of them, therefore,
took their stations within close rifle-shot of the
deer, while the other two followed the trail of
the hunter, and waylaid the path by which he
was expected to return. McConnell, expecting
no danger, rode carelessly along the path, which
the two scouts were watching, until he had
come within view of the deer, when he was
fired upon by the whole party, and his horse
killed. While laboring to extricate himself
from the dying animal, he was seized by his
enemies, instantly overpowered, and borne off
as a prisoner.

"His captors, however, seemed to be a merry,
good-natured set of fellows, and permitted him to
accompany them unbound, and, what was rather
extraordinary, allowed him to retain his gun
and hunting accouterments. He accompanied
them with great apparent cheerfulness through
the day, and displayed his dexterity in shooting

deer for the use of the company, until they began to regard him with great partiality. Having traveled with them in this manner for several days, they at length reached the banks of the Ohio River. Heretofore the Indians had taken the precaution to bind him at night, although not very securely; but, on that evening, he remonstrated with them on the subject, and complained so strongly of the pain which the cords gave him, that they merely wrapped the buffalo tug loosely around his wrists, and having tied it in an easy knot, and attached the extremities of the rope to their own bodies in order to prevent his moving without awakening them, they very composedly went to sleep, leaving the prisoner to follow their example or not, as he pleased.

"McConnell determined to effect his escape that night if possible, as on the following night they would cross the river, which would render it much more difficult. He therefore lay quietly until near midnight, anxiously ruminating upon the best means of effecting his object. Accidentally casting his eyes in the direction of his feet, they fell upon the glittering blade of a knife, which had escaped its sheath, and was now lying near the feet of one of the Indians. To reach it with his hands, without disturbing the two Indians to whom he was fastened, was impossible, and it was very hazardous to attempt to draw it up with his feet. This, however, he attempted. With much difficulty he grasped the blade between his toes, and, after repeated and long-continued efforts, succeeded at length in bringing it within reach of his hands.

"To cut his cords was then but the work of a moment, and gradually and silently extricating his person from the arms of the Indians, he walked to the fire and sat down. He saw that his work was but half done. That if he should attempt to return home without destroying his enemies, he would assuredly be pursued and probably overtaken, when his fate would be certain. On the other hand, it seemed almost impossible for a single man to succeed in a conflict with five Indians, even although unarmed and asleep. He could not hope to deal a blow with his knife so silently and fatally as to destroy each one of his enemies in turn without awakening the rest. Their slumbers were proverbially light and restless ; and, if he failed with a single one, he must instantly be overpowered by the survivors. The knife, therefore, was out of the question.

" After anxious reflection for a few minutes, he formed his plan. The guns of the Indians were stacked near the fire; their knives and tomahawks were in sheaths by their sides. The latter he dared not touch for fear of awakening their owners; but the former he carefully removed, with the exception of two, and hid them in the woods, where he knew the Indians would not readily find them. He then returned to the spot where the Indians were still sleeping, perfectly ignorant of the fate preparing for them, and, taking a gun in each hand, he rested the muzzles upon a log within six feet of his victims, and, having taken deliberate aim at the head of one and the heart of another, he pulled both triggers at the same moment.

" Both shots were fatal. At the report of the guns the others sprung to their feet and stared wildly around them. McConnell, who had run instantly to the spot where the other rifles were hid, hastily seized one of them and fired at two of his enemies who happened to stand in a line with each other. The nearest fell dead, being shot through the center of the body ; the second fell also, bellowing loudly, but quickly recovering, limped off into the woods as fast as possible. The fifth, and the only one who remained unhurt, darted off like a deer, with a yell which announced equal terror and astonishment. McConnell, not wishing to fight any more such battles, selected his own rifle from the stack, and made the best of his way to Lexington, where he arrived safely within two days.

" Shortly afterward, Mrs. Dunlap, of Fayette, who had been several months a prisoner amongst the Indians on Mad River, made her escape, and returned to Lexington. She reported that the survivor returned to his tribe with a lamentable tale. He related that they had taken a fine young hunter near Lexington, and had brought him safely as far as the Ohio ;

that while encamped upon the bank of the river a large party of white men had fallen upon them in the night, and killed all his companions, together with the poor defenseless prisoner, who lay bound hand and foot, unable either to escape or resist."

In October, 1780, Boone, who had brought his family back to Kentucky, went to the Blue Licks in company with his brother. They were attacked by a party of Indians, and Daniel's brother was killed, and he himself pursued by them with the assistance of a dog. Being hard pressed, he shot this animal to prevent his barking from giving the alarm, and so escaped.

Kentucky having been divided into three counties, a more perfect organization of the militia was effected. A Colonel and a Lieutenant-Colonel were appointed for each county; those who held the first rank were Floyd, Logan, and Todd. Pope, Trigg, and Boone held the second. Clark was Brigadier-General, and commander-in-chief of all the Kentucky militia; besides which he had a small number of regulars at Fort Jefferson. Spies and scouting parties were continually employed, and a galley was constructed by Clark's order, which was furnished with light pieces of artillery. This new species of defense did not, however, take very well with the militia, who disliked serving upon the water, probably because they found their freedom of action too much circumscribed. The regulars were far too few to spare a force sufficient to man it, and soon it fell into disuse, though it is said to have been of considerable service while it was employed. Had the Kentuckians possessed such an auxiliary at the time of Byrd's invasion, it is probable that it would have been repelled. But on account of the reluctance of the militia to serve in it, this useful vessel was laid aside and left to rot.

The campaign, if we may so term it, of 1781, began very early. In March, several parties of Indians entered Jefferson County at different points, and ambushing the paths, killed four men, among whom was Colonel William Linn. Captain Whitaker, with fifteen men, pursued one of the parties. He followed their trail to the Ohio, when, supposing they had crossed over, he embarked his men in canoes to continue the pursuit. But as they were in the act of pushing off, the Indians, who were concealed in their rear, fired upon them, killing or wounding nine of the party. Notwithstanding this heavy loss, the survivors landed and put the Indians to flight. Neither the number of the savages engaged in this affair or their loss is mentioned in the narrative. In April, a station which had been settled by Squire Boone, near Shelbyville, became alarmed by the report of the appearance of Indians. After some deliberation, it was determined to remove to the settlement on Bear's Creek. While on their way thither they were attacked by a body of Indians and defeated with great loss. These are all the details of this action we have been able to find. Colonel Floyd collected twenty-five men to pursue the Indians, but, in spite of all his caution, fell into an ambuscade, which was estimated to consist of two hundred warriors. Half of Colonel Floyd's men were killed, and the survivors supposed that they had slain nine or ten of the Indians. This, however, is not probable; either the number of the In-

dians engaged, or their loss, is much exaggerated.
Colonel Floyd himself had a narrow escape,
being dismounted; he would have been made
prisoner, but for the gallant conduct of Captain
Wells, who gave him his horse, the colonel being exhausted, and ran by his side, to support
him in the saddle. These officers had formerly
been enemies, but the magnanimous behavior of
Wells on this occasion made them steadfast
friends.

" As if every month," says Marshall, " was to
furnish its distinguishing incident—in May,
Samuel McAfee and another had set out from
James McAfee's Station for a plantation at a
small distance, and when advanced about one-
fourth of a mile they were fired on; the man
fell—McAfee wheeled and ran toward the fort;
in fifteen steps he met an Indian—they each
halt and present their guns, with muzzles almost
touching—at the same instant they each pull
trigger. McAfee's gun makes clear fire, the
Indian's flashes in the pan—and he falls;
McAfee continues his retreat, but the alarm
being given, he meets his brothers, Robert and

James—the first, though cautioned, ran along
the path to see the dead Indian, by this time
several Indians had gained the path between
him and the fort. All his agility and dexterity
was now put to the test—he flies from tree to
tree, still aiming to get to the fort, but is pursued by an Indian; he throws himself over a
fence, a hundred and fifty yards from the fort,
and the Indian takes a tree—Robert, sheltered
by the fence, was soon prepared for him, and
while he puts his face by the side of the tree
to look for his object, McAfee fires his rifle at
it, and lodged the ball in his mouth—in this he
finds his death, and McAfee escapes to the
fort."

In the mean time, James McAfee was in a
situation of equal hazard and perplexity. Five
Indians, lying in ambush, fired at, but missed
him; he flies to a tree for safety, and instantly
received a fire from three or four Indians on
the other side—the bullets knock the dust about
his feet, but do him no injury; he abandons
the tree and makes good his retreat to the fort.
One white man and two Indians were killed.

Such were the incidents of Indian warfare—and such the fortunate escape of the brothers.

Other events occurred in rapid succession—the Indians appear in all directions, and with horrid yells and menacing gestures commence a fire on the fort. It was returned with spirit; the women cast the bullets—the men discharged them at the enemy. This action lasted about two hours; the Indians then withdrew. The firing had been heard, and the neighborhood roused for the fight. Major Magary, with some of his men, and others from other stations, to the number of forty, appeared on the ground soon after the Indians had retreated, and determined on pursuing them. This was accordingly done with promptitude and celerity. At the distance of a mile the enemy were overtaken, attacked, and defeated. They fled—were pursued for several miles—and completely routed. Six or seven Indians were seen dead, and others wounded. One Kentuckian was killed in the action; another mortally wounded, who died after a few days. Before the Indians entirely withdrew from the fort they killed all the cattle they saw, without making any use of them.

From this time McAfee's Station was never more attacked, although it remained for several years an exposed frontier. Nor should the remark be omitted that for the residue of the year there were fewer incidents of a hostile nature than usual.

Fort Jefferson, which had been established on the Mississippi, about five miles below the mouth of the Ohio, had excited the jealousy of the Choctaws and Chickasaws, who claimed the territory in which it was built. In order to appease them, it was deemed advisable to evacuate the post.

The hostile tribes north of the Ohio had by this time found the strength of the settlers, and saw that unless they made a powerful effort, and that speedily, they must forever relinquish all hope of reconquering Kentucky. Such an effort was determined upon for the next year; and in order to weaken the whites as much as possible, till they were prepared for it, they continued to send out small parties, to infest the settlements.

At a distance of about twelve miles from Logan's Fort was a settlement called the Montgomery Station. Most of the people were connected with Logan's family. This Station was surrounded in the night. In the morning an attack was made. Several persons were killed and others captured. A girl who escaped spread the alarm ; a messenger reached Logan's Fort, and General Logan with a strong party pursued the Indians, defeated them and recovered the prisoners.

CHAPTER XV.

News of Cornwallis's surrender—Its effects—Captain Estill's defeat—Grand army of Indians raised for the conquest of Kentucky—Simon Girty's speech—Attack on Hoy's Station —Investment of Bryant's Station—Expedient of the besieged to obtain water—Grand attack on the fort—Repulse— Regular siege commenced—Messengers sent to Lexington— Reinforcement obtained—Arrival near the fort—Ambushed and attacked—They enter the fort—Narrow escape of Girty—He proposes a capitulation—Parley—Reynolds' answer to Girty—The siege raised—Retreat of the Indians.

IN October, 1781, Cornwallis surrendered at Yorktown. This event was received in Kentucky, as in other parts of the country, with great joy. The power of Britain was supposed to be broken, or at least so much crippled, that they would not be in a condition to assist their Indian allies as they had previously done. The winter passed away quietly enough and the people were once more lulled into security from which they were again to be rudely awakened. Early in the spring the parties of the enemy recommenced their forays. Yet there was noth ing in these to excite unusual apprehensions. At first they were scarcely equal in magnitude to those of the previous year. Cattle were killed, and horses stolen, and individuals or small parties were attacked. But in May an affair occurred possessing more interest, in a military point of view, than any other in the history of Indian wars.

In the month of May a party of about twenty-five Wyandots invested Estill's Station, on the south of the Kentucky River, killed one white man, took a negro prisoner, and after destroying the cattle, retreated. Soon after the Indians disappeared, Captain Estill raised a company of twenty-five men ; with these he pursued the Indians, and on Hinkston's Fork of Licking, two miles below the Little Mountain, came within gunshot of them. They had just crossed the creek, which in that part is small, and were ascending one side as Estill's party descended the other, of two approaching hills of moderate elevation. The watercourse which lay between had produced an opening in the timber and brush, conducing to mutual discovery, while

both hills were well set with trees, interspersed
with saplings and bushes. Instantly after discovering the Indians, some of Captain Estill's
men fired at them; at first they seemed alarmed,
and made a movement like flight; but their
chief, although wounded, gave them orders to
stand and fight—on which they promptly prepared for battle by each man taking a tree and
facing his enemy, as nearly in a line as practicable. In this position they returned the fire
and entered into the battle, which they considered as inevitable, with all the fortitude and
animation of individual and concerted bravery
so remarkable in this particular tribe.

In the meantime, Captain Estill, with due
attention to what was passing on the opposite
side, checked the progress of his men at about
sixty yards distance from the foe, and gave
orders to extend their lines in front of the
Indians, to cover themselves by means of the
trees, and to fire as the object should be seen—
with a sure aim. This order, perfectly adapted
to the occasion, was executed with alacrity, as far
as circumstances would admit, and the desultory

mode of Indian fighting was thought to require. So that both sides were preparing and ready at the same time for the bloody conflict which ensued, and which proved to be singularly obstinate.

The numbers were equal; some have said, exactly twenty-five on each side. Others have mentioned that Captain Estill, upon seeing the Indians form for battle, despatched one or two of his men upon the back trail to hasten forward a small reinforcement, which he supposed was following him; and if so, it gave the Indians the superiority of numbers without producing the desired assistance, for the reinforcement never arrived.

Now were the hostile lines within rifle-shot, and the action became warm and general to their extent. Never was battle more like single combat since the use of fire-arms; each man sought his man, and fired only when he saw his mark; wounds and death were inflicted on either side—neither advancing nor retreating. The firing was deliberate; with caution they looked, but look they would, for the foe, although life itself was often the forfeit. And thus both sides firmly stood, or bravely fell, for more than an hour; upward of one-fourth of the combatants had fallen, never more to rise, on either side, and several others were wounded. Never, probably, was the native bravery or collected fortitude of men put to a test more severe. In the clangor of an ardent battle, when death is forgotten, it is nothing for the brave to die—when even cowards die like brave men—but in the cool and lingering expectation of death, none but the man of the true courage can stand. Such were those engaged in this conflict. Never was maneuvering more necessary or less practicable. Captain Estill had not a man to spare from his line, and deemed unsafe any movement in front with a view to force the enemy from their ground, because in such a movement he must expose his men, and some of them would inevitably fall before they could reach the adversary. This would increase the relative superiority of the enemy, while they would receive the survivors with tomahawk in hand, in the use of which they were practised and expert.

He clearly perceived that no advantage was to be gained over the Indians while the action was continued in their own mode of warfare. For although his men were probably the best *shooters* the Indians were undoubtedly the most expert *hiders;* that victory itself, could it have been purchased with the loss of his last man, would afford but a melancholy consolation for the loss of friends and comrades, but even of victory, without some maneuver he could not assure himself. His situation was critical, his fate seemed suspended upon the events of the minute; the most prompt expedient was demanded. He cast his eyes over the scene; the creek was before him, and seemed to oppose a charge on the enemy—retreat he could not. On the one hand he observed a valley running from the creek toward the rear of the enemy's line, and immediately combining this circumstance with the urgency of his situation, rendered the more apparently hazardous by an attempt of the Indians to extend their line and take his in flank, he determined to detach six of his men by this valley to gain the flank or rear of the enemy, while himself, with the residue, maintained his position in front.

The detachment was accordingly made under the command of Lieutenant Miller, to whom the route was shown and the order given, conformably to the above mentioned determination; un fortunately, however, it was not executed. The lieutenant, either mistaking his way or intentionally betraying his duty, his honor, and his captain, did not proceed with the requisite despatch; and the Indians, attentive to occurrences, finding out the weakened condition of their adversaries, rushed upon them and compelled a retreat after Captain Estill and eight of his men were killed. Four others were badly wounded, who, notwithstanding, made their escape; so that only nine fell into the hands of the savages, who scalped and stripped them, of course.

It was believed by the survivors of this action that one half of the Indians were killed; and this idea was corroborated by reports from their towns.

There is also a tradition that Miller, with his detachment, crossed the creek, fell in with the enemy, lost one or two of his men, and had a third or fourth wounded before he retreated.

The battle lasted two hours, and the Indian chief was himself killed immediately after he had slain Captain Estill; at least it is so stated in one account we have seen. This action had a very depressing effect upon the spirits of the Kentuckians. Yet its results to the victors were enough to make them say, with Pyrrhus, "A few more such victories, and we shall be un-done." It is very certain that the Indians would not have been willing to gain many such victories even to accomplish their darling object—the expulsion of the whites from Kentucky.

The grand army, destined to accomplish the conquest of Kentucky, assembled at Chillicothe. A detachment from Detroit reinforced them, and before setting out, Simon Girty made a speech to them, enlarging on the ingratitude of the Long-knives in rebelling against their Great Father across the water. He described in glow-ing terms the fertility of Kentucky, exhorting them to recover it from the grasp of the Long-knife before he should be too strong for them.

This speech met with the cordial approbation of the company; the army soon after took up its march for the settlements. Six hundred warriors, the flower of all the Northwestern tribes, were on their way to make what they knew must be their last effort to drive the intruders from their favorite hunting-ground.

Various parties preceded the main body, and these appearing in different places created much confusion in the minds of the inhabitants in regard to the place where the blow was to fall. An attack was made upon the garrison at Hoy's Station, and two boys were taken prisoners. The Indians, twenty in number, were pursued by Captain Holden, with seventeen men. He overtook them near the Blue Licks, (that fatal spot for the settlers,) and after a sharp conflict was obliged to retreat with the loss of four men.

News of this disaster arrived at Bryant's Station, (a post on the Elkhorn, near the road from Lexington to Maysville,) on the fourteenth of August, and the garrison prepared to march to the assistance of Hoy's Station. But in the night the main body of the enemy arrived before the fort, it having been selected as the point for the first blow.

The water for the use of the garrison was drawn from a spring at a considerable distance from the fort on the northwestern side. Near this spring the greater part of the enemy stationed themselves in ambush. On the other side of the fort a body was posted with orders to make a feint of attacking, in order to draw the attention of the garrison to that point, and give an opportunity for the main attack. At daylight the garrison, consisting of forty or fifty men, were preparing to march out, when they were startled by a heavy discharge of rifles, with an accompaniment of such yells as come only from an Indian's throat.

"All ran hastily to the picketing," says McClung, "and beheld a small party of Indians exposed to open view, firing, yelling, and making the most furious gestures. The appearance was so singular, and so different from their usual manner of fighting, that some of the more wary and experienced of the garrison instantly pronounced it a decoy party, and restrained the

young men from sallying out and attacking them,
as some of them were strongly disposed to do
The opposite side of the fort was instantly
manned, and several breaches in the picketing
rapidly repaired. Their greatest distress arose
from the prospect of suffering for water. The
more experienced of the garrison felt satisfied
that a powerful party was in ambuscade near the
spring; but at the same time they supposed that
the Indians would not unmask themselves until
the firing upon the opposite side of the fort was
returned with such warmth as to induce the
belief that the feint had succeeded.

"Acting upon this impression, and yielding to
the urgent necessity of the case, they summoned
all the women, without exception, and explaining to them the circumstances in which they
were placed, and the improbability that any injury would be offered them, until the firing had
been returned from the opposite side of the fort,
they urged them to go in a body to the spring,
and each to bring up a bucketful of water
Some of the ladies, as was natural, had no relish
for the undertaking, and asked why the men

could not bring water as well as themselves !
observing that *they* were not bullet-proof, and
that the Indians made no distinction between
male and female scalps.

"To this it was answered, that women were in
the habit of bringing water every morning to
the fort, and that if the Indians saw them engaged as usual, it would induce them to believe
that their ambuscade was undiscovered, and
that they would not unmask themselves for the
sake of firing at a few women, when they hoped,
by remaining concealed a few moments longer,
to obtain complete possession of the fort. That
if men should go down to the spring, the Indians
would immediately suspect that something was
wrong, would despair of succeeding by ambuscade, and would instantly rush upon them, follow them into the fort, or shoot them down at
the spring. The decision was soon over.

"A few of the boldest declared their readiness
to brave the danger ; and the younger and more
timid rallying in the rear of these veterans, they
all marched down in a body to the spring, within
point-blank shot of more than five hundred In-

dian warriors. Some of the girls could not help betraying symptoms of terror, but the married women, in general, moved with a readiness and composure which completely deceived the Indians. Not a shot was fired. The party were permitted to fill their buckets, one after another, without interruption; and although their steps became quicker and quicker, on their return, and when near the gate of the fort, degenerated into a rather unmilitary celerity, attended with some little crowding in passing the gate, yet not more than one-fifth of the water was spilled, and the eyes of the youngest had not dilated to more than double their ordinary size.

"Being now amply supplied with water, they sent out thirteen young men to attack the decoy party, with orders to fire with great rapidity, and make as much noise as possible, but not to pursue the enemy too far, while the rest of the garrison took post on the opposite side of the fort, cocked their guns, and stood in readiness to receive the ambuscade as soon as it was unmasked. The firing of the light parties on the Lexington road was soon heard, and quickly be came sharp and serious, gradually becoming more distant from the fort. Instantly, Girty sprung up at the head of his five hundred warriors, and rushed rapidly upon the western gate, ready to force his way over the undefended palisades. Into this immense mass of dusky bodies, the garrison poured several rapid volleys of rifle balls with destructive effect. Their consternation may be imagined. With wild cries they dispersed on the right and left, and in two minutes not an Indian was to be seen. At the same time, the party who had sallied out on the Lexington road, came running into the fort at the opposite gate, in high spirits, and laughing heartily at the success of their maneuver.

"After this repulse, the Indians commenced the attack in regular form, that is, regular Indian form, for they had no cannon, which was a great oversight and one which we would not have expected them to make, after witnessing the terror with which they had inspired the Kentuckians in Byrd's invasion.

"Two men had left the garrison immediately upon discovering the Indians, to carry the news to Lexington and demand succor. On arriving at that place they found the men had mostly gone to Hoy's Station. The couriers pursued, and overtaking them, quickly brought them back. Sixteen horsemen, and forty or fifty on foot, started to the relief of Bryant's Station, and arrived before that place at two o'clock in the afternoon.

"To the left of the long and narrow lane, where the Maysville and Lexington road now runs, there were more than one hundred acres of green standing corn. The usual road from Lexington to Bryant's ran parallel to the fence of this field, and only a few feet distant from it. On the opposite side of the road was a thick wood. Here more than three hundred Indians lay in ambush, within pistol-shot of the road, awaiting the approach of the party. The horsemen came in view at a time when the firing had ceased and everything was quiet. Seeing no enemy and hearing no noise, they entered the lane at a gallop, and were instantly saluted with a shower of rifle-balls, from each side, at the distance of ten paces.

"At the first shot the whole party set spurs to their horses, and rode at full speed through a rolling fire from either side, which continued for several hundred yards, but owing partly to the furious rate at which they rode, partly to the clouds of dust raised by the horses' feet, they all entered the fort unhurt. The men on foot were less fortunate. They were advancing through the corn-field, and might have reached the fort in safety but for their eagerness to succor their friends. Without reflecting that, from the weight and extent of the fire, the enemy must have been ten times their number, they ran up with inconsiderate courage to the spot where the firing was heard, and there found themselves cut off from the fort, and within pistol-shot of more than three hundred savages.

"Fortunately the Indians' guns had just been discharged, and they had not yet had leisure to reload. At the sight of this brave body of footmen, however, they raised a hideous yell, and rushed upon them, tomahawk in hand. Nothing but the high corn and their loaded rifles could have saved them from destruc

tion. The Indians were cautious in rushing
upon a loaded rifle with only a tomahawk, and
when they halted to load their pieces, the Kentuckians ran with great rapidity, turning and
dodging through the corn in every direction.
Some entered the wood and escaped through
the thickets of cane, some were shot down in
the corn-field, others maintained a running
fight, halting occasionally behind trees and
keeping the enemy at bay with their rifles; for,
of all men, the Indians are generally the most
cautious in exposing themselves to danger. A
stout, active, young fellow was so hard pressed
by Girty and several savages, that he was compelled to discharge his rifle (however unwilling,
having no time to reload it), and Girty fell.

"It happened, however, that a piece of thick
sole-leather was in his shot-pouch at the time,
which received the ball, and preserved his life,
although the force of the blow felled him to
the ground. The savages halted upon his fall,
and the young man escaped. Although the
skirmish and the race lasted more than an hour,
during which the corn-field presented a scene

of turmoil and bustle which can scarcely be conceived, yet very few lives were lost. Only six of the white men were killed and wounded, and probably still fewer of the enemy, as the whites never fired until absolutely necessary, but reserved their loads as a check upon the enemy. Had the Indians pursued them to Lexington, they might have possessed themselves of it without resistance, as there was no force there to oppose them; but after following the fugitives for a few hundred yards, they returned to the hopeless siege of the fort." *

The day was nearly over, and the Indians were discouraged. They had made no perceptible impression upon the fort, but had sustained a severe loss; the country was aroused, and they feared to find themselves outnumbered in their turn. Girty determined to attempt to frighten them into a capitulation. For this purpose he cautiously approached the works, and suddenly showed himself on a large stump, from which he addressed the garrison. After extolling their valor, he assured them that their resistance

* McClung.

was useless, as he expected his artillery shortly, when their fort would be crushed without difficulty. He promised them perfect security for their lives if they surrendered, and menaced them with the usual inflictions of Indian rage if they refused. He concluded by asking if they knew him. The garrison of course gave no credit to the promises of good treatment contained in this speech. They were too well acquainted with the facility with which such pledges were given and violated; but the mention of cannon was rather alarming, as the expedition of Colonel Byrd was fresh in the minds of all. None of the leaders made any answer to Girty, but a young man by the name of Reynolds took upon himself to reply to it. In regard to the question of Girty, "Whether the garrison knew him?" he said:

"'That he was very well known; that he himself had a worthless dog, to which he had given the name of "Simon Girty," in consequence of his striking resemblance to the man of that name; that if he had either artillery or reinforcements, he might bring them up and be d——d;

that if either himself, or any of the naked rascals with him, found their way into the fort, they would disdain to use their guns against them, but would drive them out again with switches, of which they had collected a great number for that purpose alone; and finally he declared that they also expected reinforcements; that the whole country was marching to their assistance; that if Girty and his gang of murderers remained twenty-four hours longer before the fort, their scalps would be found drying in the sun upon the roofs of their cabins.' " *

Girty affected much sorrow for the inevitable destruction which he assured the garrison awaited them, in consequence of their obstinacy. All idea of continuing the siege was now abandoned. The besiegers evacuated their camp that very night; and with so much precipitation, that meat was left roasting before the fires. Though we cannot wonder at this relinquishing of a long-cherished scheme when we consider the character of the Indians, yet it would be impossible to account for the appear-

* McClung.

ance of precipitancy, and even terror, with which their retreat was accompanied, did we not perceive it to be the first of a series of similar artifices, designed to draw on their enemies to their own destruction. There was nothing in the circumstances to excite great apprehensions. To be sure, they had been repulsed in their attempt on the fort with some loss, yet this loss (thirty men) would by no means have deterred a European force of similar numbers from prosecuting the enterprise.

Girty and his great Indian army retired toward Ruddle's and Martin's Stations, on a circuitous route, toward Lower Blue Licks. They expected, however, to be pursued, and evidently desired it, as they left a broad trail behind them, and marked the trees which stood on their route with their tomahawks.*

* Frost: "Border Wars of the West." Peck: "Life of Boone." McClung: "Western Adventure."

CHAPTER XVI.

Arrival of reinforcements at Bryant's Station—Colonel Daniel Boone, his son and brother among them—Colonels Trigg, Todd, and others—Great number of commissioned officers —Consultation—Pursuit commenced without waiting for Colonel Logan's reinforcement—Indian Trail—Apprehensions of Boone and others—Arrival at the Blue Licks—Indians seen—Consultation—Colonel Boone's opinion—Rash conduct of Major McGary — Battle of Blue Licks commenced—Fierce encounter with the Indians—Israel Boone, Colonels Todd and Trigg, and Majors Harland and McBride killed—Attempt of the Indians to outflank the whites— Retreat of the whites—Colonel Boone nearly surrounded by Indians—Cuts his way through them, and returns to Bryant's Station—Great slaughter—Bravery of Netherland —Noble conduct of Reynolds in saving Captain Patterson— Loss of the whites—Colonel Boone's statement—Remarks on McGary's conduct—The fugitives meet Colonel Logan with his party — Return to the field of battle — Logan returns to Bryant's Station.

THE intelligence of the siege of Bryant's Station had spread far and wide, and the whole region round was in a state of intense excitement. The next morning after the enemy's retreat reinforcements began to arrive, and in the course of the day successive bodies of militia presented themselves, to the number of one hundred and eighty men.

Among this number was Colonel Daniel Boone, his son Israel, and his brother Samuel, with a strong party of men from Boonesborough. Colonel Stephen Trigg led a similar corps from Harrodsburg; and Colonel John Todd headed the militia from Lexington. Majors Harland, McGary, McBride, and Levi Todd were also among the arrivals.*

It is said that nearly one-third of the whole force assembled at Bryant's Station were commissioned officers, many of whom had hurried to the relief of their countrymen. This superior activity is to be accounted for by the fact that the officers were generally selected from the most active and skilful of the pioneers.

A consultation was held in a tumultuous manner, and it was determined to pursue the enemy at once. The Indians had retreated by way of the Lower Blue Licks. The pursuit was commenced without waiting for the junction of

* Peck.

Colonel Logan, who was known to be coming up with a strong reinforcement. The trail of the enemy exhibited a degree of carelessness very unusual in an Indian retreat. Various articles were strewn along the path, as if in terror they had been abandoned. These symptoms, while they increased the ardor of the young men, excited the apprehensions of the more experienced borderers, and Boone in particular. He noticed that, amid all the signs of disorder so lavishly displayed, the Indians seemed to take even unusual care to conceal their numbers by contracting their camp. It would seem that the Indians had rather overdone their stratagem. It was very natural to those not much experienced in Indian warfare to suppose that the articles found strewn along the road had been abandoned in the hurry of flight; but when they found that the utmost pains had been taken to point out the way to them by chopping the trees, one would have thought that the rawest among them, who had only spent a few months on the border, could have seen through so transparent an artifice. But these indications

were disregarded in the desire felt to punish
the Indians for their invasion.

Nothing was seen of the enemy till the Kentuckians reached the Blue Licks. Here, just
as they arrived at Licking River, a few Indians
were seen on the other side, retreating without
any appearance of alarm. The troops now
made a halt, and the officers held a consultation
to determine on the course to be pursued.
Colonel Daniel Boone, on being appealed to as
the most experienced person present, gave his
opinion as follows :

" That their situation was critical and deli-
cate; that the force opposed to them was undoubtedly numerous and ready for battle, as
might readily be seen from the leisurely retreat
of the few Indians who had appeared upon the
crest of the hill; that he was well acquainted
with the ground in the neighborhood of the
Licks, and was apprehensive than an ambuscade
was formed at the distance of a mile in advance,
where two ravines, one upon each side of the
ridge, ran in such a manner that a concealed
enemy might assail them at once both in front

and flank before they were apprized of the danger.

"It would be proper, therefore, to do one of two things : either to await the arrival of Logan, who was now undoubtedly on his march to join them ; or, if it was determined to attack without delay, that one-half of their number should march up the river, which there bends in an elliptical form, cross at the rapids, and fall upon the rear of the enemy, while the other division attacked them in front. At any rate, he strongly urged the necessity of reconnoitering the ground carefully before the main body crossed the river." *

McClung, in his "Western Adventures," doubts whether the plan of operation proposed by Colonel Boone would have been more successful than that actually adopted, suggesting that the enemy would have cut them off in detail, as at Estill's defeat.

But before the officers could come to any conclusion, Major McGary dashed into the river on horseback, calling on all who were not cowards

* McClung.

to follow. The next moment the whole of the
party were advancing to the attack with the
greatest ardor, but without any order whatever.
Horse and foot struggled through the river together, and, without waiting to form, rushed up
the ascent from the shore.

"Suddenly," says McClung, "the van halted.
They had reached the spot mentioned by Boone,
where the two ravines head, on each side of the
ridge. Here a body of Indians presented themselves, and attacked the van. McGary's party
instantly returned the fire but under great disadvantage. They were upon a bare and open
ridge; the Indians in a bushy ravine. The
center and rear, ignorant of the ground, hurried
up to the assistance of the van, but were soon
stopped by a terrible fire from the ravine which
flanked them. They found themselves enclosed
as if in the wings of a net, destitute of proper
shelter, while the enemy were in a great measure
covered from their fire. Still, however, they
maintained their ground. The action became
warm and bloody. The parties gradually
closed, the Indians emerged from the ravine,

and the fire became mutually destructive. The officers suffered dreadfully. Todd and Trigg in the rear, Harland, McBride and young Israel Boone in front, were already killed.

"The Indians gradually extended their line to turn the right of the Kentuckians, and cut off their retreat. This was quickly perceived by the weight of the fire from that quarter, and the rear instantly fell back in disorder, and attempted to rush through their only opening to the river. The motion quickly communicated itself to the van, and a hurried retreat became general. The Indians instantly sprung forward in pursuit, and, falling upon them with their tomahawks, made a cruel slaughter. From the battle-ground to the river the spectacle was terrible. The horsemen, generally, escaped; but the foot, particularly the van, which had advanced furthest within the wings of the net, were almost totally destroyed. Colonel Boone, after witnessing the death of his son and many of his dearest friends, found himself almost entirely surrounded at the very commencement of the retreat.

"Several hundred Indians were between him and the ford, to which the great mass of the fugitives were bending their flight, and to which the attention of the savages was principally directed. Being intimately acquainted with the ground, he, together with a few friends, dashed into the ravine which the Indians had occupied, but which most of them had now left to join in the pursuit. After sustaining one or two heavy fires, and baffling one or two small parties who pursued him for a short distance, he crossed the river below the ford by swimming, and, entering the wood at a point where there was no pursuit, returned by a circuitous route to Bryant's Station. In the meantime the great mass of the victors and vanquished crowded the bank of the ford.

"The slaughter was great in the river. The ford was crowded with horsemen and foot and Indians, all mingled together. Some were compelled to seek a passage above by swimming; some who could not swim were overtaken and killed at the edge of the water. A man by the name of Netherland, who had formerly been

strongly suspected of cowardice, here displayed
a coolness and presence of mind equally noble
and unexpected. Being finely mounted, he had
outstripped the great mass of fugitives, and
crossed the river in safety. A dozen or twenty
horsemen accompanied him, and, having placed
the river between them and the enemy, showed
a disposition to continue their flight, without
regard to the safety of their friends who were
on foot and still struggling with the current.

"Netherland instantly checked his horse, and
in a loud voice called upon his companions to
halt, fire upon the Indians, and save those who
were still in the stream. The party instantly
obeyed, and, facing about, poured a close and
fatal discharge of rifles upon the foremost of
the pursuers. The enemy instantly fell back
from the opposite bank, and gave time for the
harassed and miserable footmen to cross in
safety. The check, however, was but momentary. Indians were seen crossing in great numbers above and below, and the flight again
became general. Most of the foot left the great
buffalo track, and plunging into the thickets,

escaped by a circuitous route to Bryant's Station."

The pursuit was kept up for twenty miles, though with but little success. In the flight from the scene of action to the river, young Reynolds (the same who replied to Girty's summons at Bryant's Station), on horseback, overtook Captain Patterson on foot. This officer had not recovered from the effects of wounds received on a former occasion, and was altogether unable to keep up with the rest of the fugitives.

Reynolds immediately dismounted, and gave the captain his horse. Continuing his flight on foot, he swam the river, but was made prisoner by a party of Indians. He was left in charge of a single Indian, whom he soon knocked down, and so escaped. For the assistance he so gallantly rendered him, Captain Patterson rewarded Reynolds with a present of two hundred acres of land.

Sixty whites were killed in this battle of the Blue Licks, and seven made prisoners. Colonel Boone, in his Autobiography, says that he was informed that the Indian loss in killed was four more than that of the Kentuckians, and that the former put four of the prisoners to death, to make the numbers equal. But this account does not seem worthy of credit, when we consider the vastly superior numbers of the Indians, their advantage of position, and the disorderly manner in which the Kentuckians advanced. If this account is true, the loss of the Indians in the actual battle must have been much greater than that of their opponents, many of the latter having been killed in the pursuit.

As the loss of the Kentuckians on this oc casion, the heaviest they had ever sustained, was undoubtedly caused by rashness, it becomes our duty, according to the established usage of historians, to attempt to show where the fault lies. The conduct of McGary, which brought on the action, appears to be the most culpable. He never denied the part which is generally attributed to him, but justified himself by say· ing that while at Bryant's Station, he had advised waiting for Logan, but was met with the charge of cowardice. He believed that Todd and Trigg were jealous of Logan, who was the senior colonel, and would have taken the command had he come up. This statement he made to a gentleman several years after the battle took place. He said also to the same person, that when he found them hesitating in the presence of the enemy, he " burst into a passion," called them cowards, and dashed into the river as before narrated. If this account be true, it may somewhat palliate, but certainly not justify the action.

Before the fugitives reached Bryant's Station they met Logan advancing with his detachment. The exaggerated accounts he received of the slaughter induced him to return to the above-mentioned place. On the next morning all who had escaped from the battle were assembled, when Logan found himself at the head of four hundred and fifty men. With this force, accompanied by Colonel Boone, he set out for the scene of action, hoping that the enemy, encouraged by their success, would await his arrival. But when he reached the field he found it deserted. The bodies of the slain Kentuckians, frightfully mangled, were strewed over the ground. After collecting and interring these, Logan and Boone, finding they could do nothing more, returned to Bryant's Station, where they disbanded the troops.

"By such rash men as McGary," says Mr. Peck,* "Colonel Boone was charged with want of courage, when the result proved his superior wisdom and foresight. All the testimony gives Boone credit for his sagacity and correctness in judgment before the action and his coolness and self-possession in covering the retreat. His report of this battle to Benjamin Harrison, Governor of Virginia, is one of the few documents that remain from his pen."

"*Boone's Station, Fayette County,
August 30th,* 1782.

"Sir : Present circumstances of affairs cause me to write to your Excellency as follows: On the 16th instant a large number of Indians, with some white men, attacked one of our fron-

* "Life of Boone," p. 130.

tier Stations, known by the name of Bryant's
Station. The siege continued from about sunrise till about ten o'clock the next day, when they
marched off. Notice being given to the neighboring Stations, we immediately raised one
hundred and eighty-one horse, commanded by
Colonel John Todd, including some of the Lincoln County militia, commanded by Colonel
Trigg, and pursued about forty miles.

"On the 19th instant we discovered the
enemy lying in wait for us. On this discovery,
we formed our columns into one single line, and
marched up in their front within about forty
yards, before there was a gun fired. Colonel
Trigg commanded on the right, myself on the
left, Major McGary in the center, and Major
Harlan the advanced party in front. From the
manner in which we had formed, it fell to my
lot to bring on the attack. This was done with
a very heavy fire on both sides, and extended
back of the line to Colonel Trigg, where the
enemy were so strong they rushed up and broke
the right wing at the first fire. Thus the enemy
got in our rear, with the loss of seventy-seven of

our men and twelve wounded. Afterward we were reinforced by Colonel Logan, which made our force four hundred and sixty men. We marched again to the battle-ground; but finding the enemy had gone, we proceeded to bury the dead.

"We found forty-three on the ground, and many lay about, which we could not stay to find, hungry and weary as we were, and somewhat dubious that the enemy might not have gone off quite. By the signs, we thought that the Indians had exceeded four hundred; while the whole of this militia of the county does not amount to more than one hundred and thirty. From these facts your Excellency may form an idea of our situation.

"I know that your own circumstances are critical; but are we to be wholly forgotten? I hope not. I trust about five hundred men may be sent to our assistance immediately. If these shall be stationed as our county lieutenants shall deem necessary, it may be the means of saving our part of the country; but if they are placed under the direction of General Clark, they will

be of little or no service to our settlement.
The Falls lie one hundred miles west of us, and
the Indians northeast; while our men are frequently called to protect them.   I have encouraged the people in this county all that I could;
but I can no longer justify them or myself to risk
our lives here under such extraordinary hazards.
The inhabitants of this county are very much
alarmed at the thoughts of the Indians bringing another campaign into our country this fall.
If this should be the case, it will break up these
settlements.   I hope, therefore, your Excellency
will take the matter into consideration and send
us some relief as quick as possible.

"These are my sentiments, without consulting
any person.   Colonel Logan will, I expect, immediately send you an express, by whom I
humbly request your Excellency's answer.   In
the meanwhile, I remain,

                            "DANIEL BOONE."

CHAPTER XVII.

The Indians return home from the Blue Licks—They attack the settlements in Jefferson County—Affair at Simpson's Creek—General Clark's expedition to the Indian country—Colonel Boone joins it—Its effect—Attack of the Indians on the Crab Orchard settlement—Rumor of intended invasion by the Cherokees—Difficulties about the treaty with Great Britain—Hostilities of the Indians generally stimulated by renegade whites—Simon Girty—Causes of his hatred of the whites—Girty insulted by General Lewis—Joins the Indians at the battle of Point Pleasant—Story of his rescuing Simon Kenton—Crawford's expedition, and the Burning of Crawford—Close of Girty's career.

MOST of the Indians who had taken part in the battle of the Blue Licks, according to their custom, returned home to boast of their victory, thus abandoning all the advantages which might have resulted to them from following up their success. Some of them, however, attacked the settlements in Jefferson County, but they were prevented from doing much mischief by the vigilance of the inhabitants. They succeeded, however, in breaking up a small settlement on Simpson's

Creek. This they attacked in the night, while the men, wearied by a scout of several days, were asleep. The enemy entered the houses before their occupants were fully aroused. Notwith-standing this, several of the men defended themselves with great courage. Thompson Randolph killed several Indians before his wife and infant were struck down at his side, when he escaped with his remaining child through the roof. On reaching the ground he was assailed by two of the savages, but he beat them off, and escaped. Several women escaped to the woods, and two were secreted under the floor of a cabin, where they remained undiscovered. Still the Indians captured quite a number of women and children, some of whom they put to death on the road home. The rest were liberated the next year upon the conclusion of peace with the English.

General George Rogers Clark proposed a re-taliatory expedition into the Indian country, and, to carry out the plan, called a council of the superior officers. The council agreed to his plan, and preparations were made to raise the requisite number of troops by drafting, if there should be any deficiency of volunteers. But it was not found necessary to resort to compulsory measures, both men and supplies for the expedition were raised without difficulty. The troops to the number of one thousand, all mounted, assembled at Bryant's Station, and the Falls of the Ohio, from whence the two detachments marched under Logan and Floyd to the mouth of the Licking, where General Clark assumed the command. Colonel Boone took part in this expedition; but probably as a volunteer. He is not mentioned as having a separate command.

The history of this expedition, like most others of the same nature, possesses but little interest. The army with all the expedition they could make, and for which the species of force was peculiarly favorable, failed to surprise the Indians. These latter opposed no resistance of importance to the advance of the army. Occasionally, a straggling party would fire upon the Kentuckians, but never waited to receive a similar compliment in return. Seven Indians were taken prisoners and three or four killed; one of them an old chief, too infirm to fly, was

killed by Major McGary. The towns of the
Indians were burnt and their fields devastated.
The expedition returned to Kentucky with the
loss of four men, two of whom were accidentally
killed by their own comrades.

This invasion, though apparently so barren of
result, is supposed to have produced a beneficial
effect, by impressing the Indians with the numbers and courage of the Kentuckians. They
appear from this time to have given up the expectation of reconquering the country, and confined their hostilities to the rapid incursions of
small bands.

During the expedition of Clark, a party of
Indians penetrated to the Crab Orchard settlement. They made an attack upon a single
house, containing only a woman, a negro man,
and two or three children. One of the Indians,
who had been sent in advance to reconnoiter,
seeing the weakness of the garrison, thought to
get all the glory of the achievement to himself.

He boldly entered the house and seized the
negro, who proving strongest threw him on the

floor, when the woman despatched him with an ax. The other Indians, coming up, attempted to force open the door, which had been closed by the children during the scuffle. There was no gun in the house, but the woman seized an old barrel of one, and thrust the muzzle through the logs, at which the Indians retreated.

The year 1783 passed away without any disturbance from the Indians, who were restrained by the desertion of their allies the British. In 1784, the southern frontier of Kentucky was alarmed by the rumor of an intended invasion by the Cherokees, and some preparations were made for an expedition against them, which fell through, however, because there was no authority to carry it on. The report of the hostility of the Cherokees proved to be untrue.

Meanwhile difficulties arose in performance of the terms of the treaty between England and the United States. They appear to have originated in a dispute in regard to an article contained in the treaty providing that the British army should not carry away with them any negroes or other property belonging to the American inhabitants. In consequence of what they deemed an infraction of this article, the Virginians refused to comply with another, which stipulated for the repeal of acts prohibit. ing the collection of debts due to British sub· jects. The British, on the other hand, refused to evacuate the western posts till this article was complied with. It was natural that the intercourse which had always existed between the Indians and the garrison of these posts, during the period they had acted as allies, should continue, and it did.

In the unwritten history of the difficulties of the United States Government with the Indian tribes within her established boundaries, nothing appears clearer than this truth: that the fierce and sanguinary resistance of the aborigines to the encroachments of the Anglo-Americans has ever been begun and continued more through the instigations of outlawed white men, who had sought protection among them from the arm of the law or the knife of individual vengeance, and been adopted into their tribes,

than from the promptings of their own judgments, their disregard of death, their thirst for
the blood of their oppressors, or their love of
country.[*]

That their sense of wrong has at all times
been keen, their hate deadly, and their bravery
great, is a fact beyond dispute; and that they
have prized highly their old hunting-grounds,
and felt a warm and lively attachment to their
beautiful village sites, and regarded with
especial veneration the burial-places of their
fathers, their whole history attests; but of their
own weakness in war, before the arms and
numbers of their enemies, they must have been
convinced at a very early period; and they
were neither so dull in apprehension, nor so
weak in intellect, as not soon to have perceived
the utter hopelessness, and felt the mad folly
of a continued contest with their invaders.
Long before the settlement of the whites upon
this continent, the Indians had been subject to
bloody and exterminating wars among themselves; and such conflicts had generally resulted

[*] Gallagher. "Hesperian," vol. i. p. 343.

in the flight of the weaker party towards the West, and the occupancy of their lands by the conquerors. Many of the tribes had a tradition among them, and regarded it as their unchangeable destiny, that they were to journey from the rising to the setting sun, on their way to the bright waters and the green forests of the "Spirit Land," and the working out of this destiny seems apparent, if not in the location, course, and character of the tumuli and other remains of the great aboriginal nations of whom even tradition furnishes no account, certainly in what we know of the history of the tribes found on the Atlantic coast by the first European settlers.

It seems fairly presumable, from our knowledge of the history and character of the North American Indians, that had they been left to the promptings of their own judgments, and been influenced only by the deliberations of their own councils, they would, after a brief, but perhaps most bloody, resistance to the encroachments of the whites, have bowed to what would have struck their untutored minds as an

inevitable destiny, and year after year flowed
silently, as the European wave pressed upon
them, further and further into the vast
wildernesses of the mighty West. But left
to their own judgments, or their own deliberations, they never have been. Early armed
by renegade white men with European weapons, and taught the improvement of their own
rude instruments of warfare, and instigated not
only to oppose the strides of their enemies
after territory, but to commit depredations upon
their settlements, and to attempt to chastise
them at their very thresholds, they drew down
upon themselves the wrath of a people which
is not slow to anger, nor easily appeased; and
as far back as the Revolution, if not as the
colonizing of Massachusetts, their breasts were
filled with a hatred of the whites, deadly
and unslumbering. Through all our subsequent transactions with them, this feeling has
been increasing in magnitude and intensity:
and recent events have carried it to a pitch
which will render it enduring forever, perhaps
not in its activity, but certainly in its bitterness.

Whether more amicable relations with the whites during the first settlements made upon this continent by the Europeans would have changed materially the ultimate destiny of the aboriginal tribes, is a question about which diversities of opinion may well be entertained; but it is not to be considered here.

The fierce, and bloody, and continuous opposition which the Indians have made from the first to the encroachments of the Anglo-Americans is matter of history: and close scrutiny will show that the great instigators of that opposition have always, or nearly so, been *renegade white men.* Scattered through the tribes east of the Alleghanies, before and during the American Revolution, there were many such miscreants. Among the Western tribes, during the early settlement of Kentucky and Ohio, and at the period of the last war with Great Britain, there were a number, some of them men of talent and great activity. One of the boldest and most notorious of these latter was one whom we have had frequent occasion to mention, SIMON GIRTY—for many years the scourge of the infant settlements in the West, the terror of women, and the bugaboo of children. This man was an adopted member of the great Wyandot nation, among whom he ranked high as an expert hunter, a brave warrior, and a powerful orator. His influence extended through all the tribes of the West, and was generally exerted to incite the Indians to expeditions against the "Stations" of Kentucky, and to acts of cruelty to their white prisoners. The bloodiest counsel was usually his; his was the voice which was raised loudest against his countrymen, who were preparing the way for the introduction of civilization and Christianity into this glorious region; and in all great attacks upon the frontier settlements he was one of the prime movers, and among the prominent leaders.

Of the causes of that venomous hatred, which rankled in the bosom of Simon Girty against his countrymen, we have two or three versions: such as, that he early imbibed a feeling of contempt and abhorrence of civilized life, from the brutality of his father, the lapse from virtue of

his mother, and the corruptions of the com-
munity in which he had passed his boyhood;
that, while acting with bravery against the
Indians on the Virginia border, he was stung to
the quick, and deeply offended by the appointment to a station over his head, of one who was
his junior in years, and had rendered nothing
like his services to the frontiers; and that, when
attached as a scout to Dunmore's expedition, an
indignity was heaped upon him which thoroughly soured his nature, and drove him to the
Indians, that he might more effectually execute
a vengeance which he swore to wreak. The
last reason assigned for his defection and animosity is the most probable of the three, rests
upon good authority, and seems sufficient, his
character considered, to account for his desertion
and subsequent career among the Indians.

The history of the indignity alluded to, as it has
reached the writer * from one who was associated
with Girty and a partaker in it, is as follows:
The two were acting as scouts in the expedition
set on foot by Governor Dunmore, of Virginia,

* Gallagher.

in the year 1774, against the Indian towns of
Ohio. The two divisions of the force raised for
this expedition, the one commanded by Governor
Dunmore in person, the other by General
Andrew Lewis, were by the orders of the Governor to form a junction at Point Pleasant, where
the Great Kanawha empties into the Ohio. At
this place, General Lewis arrived with his command on the eleventh or twelfth of September;
but after remaining here two or three weeks in
anxious expectation of the approach of the other
division, he received despatches from the Governor informing him that Dunmore had changed
his plan, and determined to march at once
against the villages on the Scioto, and ordering
him to cross the Ohio immediately and join him
as speedily as possible. It was during the delay
at the Point that the incident occurred which is
supposed to have had such a tremendous influence upon Girty's after-life. He and his associate scout had rendered some two or three
months' services, for which they had as yet
drawn no part of their pay; and in their present
idleness they discovered means of enjoyment, of

which they had not money to avail themselves. In this strait they called upon General Lewis in person at his quarters and demanded their pay. For some unknown cause this was refused, which produced a slight murmuring on the part of the applicants, when General Lewis cursed them, and struck them several severe blows over their heads with his cane. Girty's associate was not much hurt; but he himself was so badly wounded on the forehead or temple that the blood streamed down his cheek and side to the floor. He quickly turned to leave the apartment, but, on reaching the door, wheeled round, planted his feet firmly upon the sill, braced an arm against either side of the frame, fixed his keen eyes unflinchingly upon the general, uttered the exclamation, "*By God, sir, your quarters shall swim in blood for this!*" and instantly disappeared beyond pursuit.

General Lewis was not much pleased with the sudden and apparently causeless change which Governor Dunmore had made in the plan of the expedition. Nevertheless, he immediately prepared to obey the new orders, and had given directions for the construction of rafts upon which to cross the Ohio, when, before day-light on the morning of the 10th of October, some of the scouts suddenly entered the encampment with the information that an immense body of Indians was just at hand, hastening upon the Point. This was the force of the brave and skilful chief Cornstalk, whose genius and valor were so conspicuous on that day, throughout the whole of which raged the hardly-contested and most bloody *Battle of the Point.* Girty had fled from General Lewis immediately to the chief Cornstalk, forsworn his white nature, and leagued himself with the Red-man forever; and with the Indians he was now advancing, under the cover of night, to surprise the Virginian camp. At the distance of only a mile from the Point Cornstalk was met by a detachment of the Virginians, under the command of Colonel Charles Lewis, a brother of the general; and here, about sunrise on the 10th of October, 1774, commenced one of the longest, severest, and bloodiest battles ever fought upon the Western frontiers. It terminated, as we have seen, about sunset, with the defeat of the Indians, it is true, but with a loss to the whites which carried mourning into many a mansion of the Old Dominion, and which was keenly felt throughout the country at the time, and remembered with sorrow long after.

Girty having thrown himself among the Indians, as has been related, and embraced their cause, now retreated with them into the interior of Ohio, and ever after followed their fortunes without swerving. On arriving at the towns of the Wyandots, he was adopted into that tribe, and established himself at Upper Sandusky. Being active, of a strong constitution, fearless in the extreme, and at all times ready to join their war parties, he soon become very popular among his new associates, and a man of much consequence. He was engaged in most of the expeditions against the frontier settlements of Pennsylvania and Virginia—always brave and always cruel—till the year 1778, when occurred an incident which, as it the only bright spot apparent on the whole dark career of the renegade, shall be related with some particularity.

Girty happened to be at Lower Sandusky this year, when Kenton—known at that period as Simon Butler—was brought in to be executed by a party of Indians who had made him a prisoner on the banks of the Ohio. Years before, Kenton and Girty had been bosom companions at Fort Pitt, and served together subsequently in the commencement of Dunmore's expedition; but the victim was already blackened for the stake, and the renegade failed to recognize in him his former associate. Girty had at this time but just returned from an expedition against the frontier of Pennsylvania which had been less successful than he had anticipated, and was enraged by disappointment. He, therefore, as soon as Kenton was brought into the village, began to give vent to a portion of his spleen by cuffing and kicking the prisoner, whom he eventually knocked down. He knew that Kenton had come from Kentucky; and this harsh treatment was bestowed in part, it is thought, to frighten the prisoner into answers of such questions as he might wish to ask him. He then inquired how many men there were in Kentucky. Kenton could not answer this question, but ran over the names and ranks of such of the officers as he at the time recollected. "Do you know William Stewart?" asked Girty. "Perfectly well," replied Kenton; "he is an old and intimate acquaintance." "Ah! what is *your* name, then?" "Simon Butler," answered Kenton; and on the instant of this announcement the hardened renegade caught his old comrade by the hand, lifted him from the ground, pressed him to his bosom, asked his forgiveness for having treated him so brutally, and promised to do everything in his power to save his life and set him at liberty. "Syme!" said he, weeping like a child, "you are condemned to die, but it shall go hard with me, I tell you, but I will save you from *that.*"

There have been various accounts given of this interesting scene, and all agree in representing Girty as having been deeply affected, and moved for the moment to penitence and tears. The foundation of McClung's detail of the speeches made upon the occasion was a manuscript dictated by Kenton himself a number of years before his death. From this writer we therefore quote :

" As soon as Girty heard the name he became strongly agitated ; and, springing from his seat, he threw his arms around Kenton's neck, and embraced him with much emotion. Then turning to the assembled warriors, who remained astonished spectators of this extraordinary scene, he addressed them in a short speech, which the deep earnestness of his tone, and the energy of his gesture, rendered eloquent. He informed them that the prisoner, whom they had just condemned to the stake, was his ancient comrade and bosom friend ; that they had traveled the same warpath, slept upon the same blanket and dwelt in the same wigwam. He entreated them to have compassion on his feelings—to spare him the agony of witnessing the torture of an old friend by the hands of his adopted brothers, and not to refuse so trifling a favor as the life of a white man to the earnest intercession of one who had proved, by three years' faithful service, that he was sincerely and zealously devoted to the cause of the Indians.

"The speech was listened to in unbroken silence. As soon as he had finished, several chiefs expressed their approbation by a deep guttural interjection, while others were equally as forward in making known their objections to the proposal. They urged that his fate had al-ready been determined in a large and solemn council, and that they would be acting like squaws to change their minds every hour. They insisted upon the flagrant misdemeanors of Kenton—that he had not only stolen their horses, but had flashed his gun at one of their young men—that it was vain to suppose that so bad a man could ever become an Indian at heart, like their brother Girty—that the Ken-tuckians were all alike—very bad people—and ought to be killed as fast as they were taken—and finally, they observed that many of their people had come from a distance, solely to assist at the torture of the prisoner, and pathetically painted the disappointment and chagrin with which they would hear that all their trouble had been for nothing.

"Girty listened with obvious impatience to

the young warriors who had so ably argued against a reprieve—and starting to his feet, as soon as the others had concluded, he urged his former request with great earnestness. He briefly, but strongly recapitulated his own serv· ices, and the many and weighty instances of attachment he had given. He asked if *he* could be suspected of partiality to the whites? When had he ever before interceded for any of that hated race? Had he not brought seven scalps home with him from the last expedition? and had he not submitted seven white prisoners that very evening to their discretion? Had he ever expressed a wish that a single captive should be saved? *This* was his first and should be his last request: for if they refused to *him*, what was never refused to the intercession of one of their natural chiefs, he would look upon himself as disgraced in their eyes, and considered as un· worthy of confidence. Which of their own natural warriors had been more zealous than himself? From what expedition had he ever shrunk?—what white man had ever seen his back? Whose tomahawk had been bloodier

than his? He would say no more. He asked
it as a first and last favor, as an evidence that
they approved of his zeal and fidelity, that the
life of his bosom friend might be spared. Fresh
speakers arose upon each side, and the debate
was carried on for an hour and a half with great
heat and energy.

"During the whole of this time, Kenton's
feelings may readily be imagined. He could
not understand a syllable of what was said.
He saw that Girty spoke with deep earnestness,
and that the eyes of the assembly were often
turned upon himself with various expressions.
He felt satisfied that his friend was pleading
for his life, and that he was violently opposed
by a large part of the council. At length the
war-club was produced, and the final vote
taken. Kenton watched its progress with thrilling emotion—which yielded to the most rapt-
urous delight, as he perceived that those who
struck the floor of the council-house were decid-
edly inferior in number to those who passed it
in silence. Having thus succeeded in his benev-
olent purpose, Girty lost no time in attending

to the comfort of his friend. He led him into his own wigwam, and from his own store gave him a pair of moccasins and leggins, a breech-cloth, a hat, a coat, a handkerchief for his neck and another for his head."

In the course of a few weeks, and after passing through some further difficulties, in which the renegade again stood by him faithfully, Kenton was sent to Detroit, from which place he effected his escape and returned to Kentucky. Girty remained with the Indians, retaining his old influence, and continuing his old career; and four years after the occurrences last detailed, in 1782, we find him a prominent figure in one of the blackest tragedies that have ever disgraced the annals of mankind. It is generally believed, by the old settlers and their immediate descendants, that the influence of Girty at this period, over the confederate tribes of the whole northwest, was almost supreme. He had, it is true, no delegated authority, and of course was powerless as regarded the final determination of any important measure; but his voice was permitted in council among the chiefs and his inflaming harangues were always listened to with delight by the young warriors. Among the sachems and other head-men, he was what may well be styled a " power behind the throne " ; and as it is well known that this unseen power is often "greater than the throne itself," it may reason-ably be presumed that Girty's influence was in reality all which it is supposed to have been. The horrible event alluded to above was the *burning of Crawford;* and as a knowledge of this dark passage in his life is necessary to a full development of the character of the renegade, an account of the incident, as much condensed as possible, will be given from the histories of the unfortunate campaign of that year.

The frontier settlements of Pennsylvania and Virginia had been greatly harassed by repeated attacks from bands of Indians under Girty and some of the Wyandot and Shawanee chiefs, dur-ing the whole period of the Revolutionary War ; and early in the spring of 1782 these savage incursions became so frequent and galling, and the common mode of fighting the Indians on the line of frontier, when forced to do so in self defense, proved so inefficient, that it was found absolutely necessary to carry the war into the country of the enemy. For this purpose an expedition against the Wyandot towns on the Sandusky was gotten up in May, and put under the command of Colonel William Crawford, a brave soldier of the Revolution. This force, amounting to upward of four hundred mounted volunteers, commenced its march through the wilderness northwest of the Ohio River, on the 25th of May, and reached the plains of the San-dusky on the 5th of June. A spirit of insubor-dination had manifested itself during the march, and on one occasion a small body of the volun-teers abandoned the expedition and returned to their homes. The disaffection which had pre-vailed on the march continued to disturb the com-mander and divide the ranks, after their arrival upon the very site (now deserted temporarily) of one of the enemy's principal towns; and the officers, yielding to the wishes of their men, had actually determined, in a hasty council, to abandon the objects of the expedition and return home, if they did not meet with the Indians in

large force in the course of another day's march.
Scarcely had this determination been announced,
however, when Colonel Crawford received intelligence from his scouts of the near approach
of a large body of the enemy. Preparations
were at once made for the engagement, which
almost instantly commenced. It was now about
the middle of the afternoon; and from this
time till dusk the firing was hot and galling on
both sides. About dark the Indians drew off
their force, when the volunteers encamped upon
the battle-ground and slept on their arms.

The next day the battle was renewed by
small detachments of the enemy, but no general
engagement took place. The Indians had
suffered severely from the close firing which ensued upon their first attack, and were now maneuvering and awaiting the arrival of reinforcements. No sooner had night closed upon this
madly spent day, than the officers assembled in
council. They were unanimous in the opinion
that the enemy, already as they thought more
numerous than their own force, was rapidly
increasing in numbers. They therefore deter-

mined, without a dissenting voice, to retreat that night, as rapidly as circumstances would permit. This resolution was at once announced to the whole body of volunteers, and the arrangements necessary to carry it into effect were immediately commenced. By nine or ten o'clock everything was in readiness—the troops properly disposed—and the retreat begun in good order. But unfortunately, says McClung, " they had scarcely moved an hundred paces, when the report of several rifles was heard in the rear, in the direction of the Indian encampment. The troops instantly became very unsteady. At length a solitary voice, in the front rank, called out that their design was discovered, and that the Indians would soon be upon them. Nothing more was necessary. The cavalry were instantly broken; and, as usual, each man endeavored to save himself as he best could. A prodigious uproar ensued, which quickly communicated to the enemy that the white men had routed themselves, and that they had nothing to do but pick up stragglers." A scene of confusion and carnage now took place which almost beggars

description. All that night and for the whole of
the next day, the work of hunting out, running
down, and butchering continued without intermission. But a relation of these sad occurrences
does not properly belong to this narrative. The
brief account of the expedition which has been
given was deemed necessary as an introduction
to the event which now claims attention.

Among the prisoners taken by the Indians
were Colonel Crawford, the commander, and
Dr. Knight, of Pittsburg, who had gone upon
the expedition as surgeon. On the 10th of
June these gentlemen were marched toward
the principal town of the Wyandots, where they
arrived the next day. Here they beheld the
mangled bodies of some of their late companions,
and were doomed to see others, yet living,
butchered before their eyes. Here, likewise,
they saw Simon Girty, who appeared to take an
infernal delight in gazing upon the dead bodies,
and viewing the tortures which were inflicted
upon the living. The features of this wretch,
who had known Colonel Crawford at Fort Pitt,
were clad in malicious smiles at beholding the

brave soldier in his present strait; and toward
Dr. Knight he conducted himself with insolence
as well as barbarity. The Colonel was soon
stripped naked, painted black, and commanded
to sit down by a large fire which was blazing
close at hand; and in this situation he was surrounded by all the old women and young boys
of the town, and severely beaten with sticks
and clubs. While this was going on, the Indians were sinking a large stake in the ground,
and building a circle of brushwood and hickory
sticks around it, with a diameter of some twelve
or fifteen feet. These preparations completed,
Crawford's hands were tied firmly behind his
back, and by his wrists he was bound to the
stake. The pile was then fired in several places,
and the quick flames curled into the air. Girty
took no part in these operations, but sat upon
his horse at a little distance, observing them
with a malignant satisfaction. Catching his
eye at the moment the pile was fired, Crawford
inquired of the renegade if the savages really
meant to burn him. Girty coldly answered
" Yes," and the Colonel calmly resigned himself

to his fate. The whole scene is minutely described in the several histories which have been
written of this unfortunate expedition; but the
particulars are too horrible to be dwelt upon
here. For more than two hours did the gallant
soldier survive at that flame-girdled stake; and
during the latter half of this time he was put
to every torture which savage ingenuity could
devise and hellish vengeance execute. Once
only did a word escape his lips. In the extremity of his agony he again caught the eye of
Girty; and he is reported to have exclaimed at
this time, "Girty! Girty! shoot me through
the heart! Do not refuse me! quick!—quick!"
And it is said that the monster merely replied,
"Don't you see I have no gun, Colonel?" then
burst into a loud laugh and turned away.
Crawford said no more; he sank repeatedly
beneath the pain and suffocation which he en-
dured, and was as often aroused by a new torture; but in a little while the "vital spark"
fled, and the black and swollen body lay sense-
less at the foot of the stake.

   Dr. Knight was now removed from the spot,

and placed under the charge of a Shawanee warrior to be taken to Chillicothe, where he was to share in the terrible fate of his late companion. The Doctor, however, was fortunate enough to effect his escape, and after wandering through the wilderness for three weeks, in a state bordering on starvation, he reached Pittsburg. He had been an eye-witness of all the tortures inflicted upon the Colonel, and subsequently published a journal of the expedition; and it is from this that the particulars have been derived of the several accounts which have been published of the *burning of Crawford.*[*]

It was not to be expected that such a man as Simon Girty could, for a great many years, maintain his influence among a people headed by chiefs and warriors like Black-Hood, Buckongahelas, Little Turtle, Tuthe, and so forth. Accordingly we find the ascendency of the renegade at its height about the period of the expedition against Bryant's Station, already described; and not long after this it began to

* Gallagher.

wane, when, discontent and disappointment in
ducing him to give way to his natural appetites,
he partook freely of all intoxicating liquors, and
in the course of a few years became a beastly
drunkard. It is believed that he at one time
seriously meditated an abandonment of the Indians and a return to the whites ; and an anecdote related by McClung, in his notice of the
emigration to Kentucky, by way of the Ohio
River, in the year 1785, would seem to give
color to this opinion. But if the intention ever
was seriously indulged, it is most likely that
fear of the treatment he would receive on being recognized in the frontier settlements, on
account of his many bloody enormities, prevented him from carrying it into effect. He remained with the Indians in Ohio till Wayne's
victory, when he forsook the scenes of his former influence and savage greatness, and established himself somewhere in Upper Canada. He
fought in the bloody engagement which terminated in the defeat and butchery of St. Clair's
army in 1791, and was at the battle of the Fallen Timbers in 1794, but he had no command in

either of those engagements, and was not at this time a man of any particular influence.

In Canada, Girty was something of a trader, but gave himself up almost wholly to intoxicating drinks, and became a perfect sot. At this time he suffered much from rheumatism and other diseases; but he had grown a great braggart, and amidst his severest pains he would entertain his associates, and all who were willing to listen, with stories of his past prowess and cruelty. He had now the most exaggerated notions of the honor attaching to the character of a great warrior; and for some years before his death his constantly-expressed wish was, that he might find an opportunity of signalizing his last years by some daring action, and die upon the field of battle. Whether sincere in this wish or not, the opportunity was afforded him. He fought with the Indians at Proctor's defeat on the Thames in 1814, and was among those who were here cut down and trodden under foot by Colonel Johnson's regiment of mounted Kentuckians.

Of the birthplace and family of Simon Girty

we have not been able to procure any satisfactory information. It is generally supposed,
from the fact that nearly all of his early companions were Virginians, that he was a native of
the Old Dominion; but one of the early pioneers (yet living in Franklin County), who knew
Girty at Pittsburg before his defection, thinks
that his native State was Pennsylvania. This
venerable gentleman is likewise of the opinion,
that it was the disappointment of not getting
an office to which he aspired that first filled
Girty's breast with hatred of the whites, and
roused in him those dark thoughts and bitter
feelings which subsequently, on the occurrence
of the first good opportunity, induced him to
desert his countrymen and league himself with
the Indians. That Girty was an applicant or
candidate for some office, and was defeated in
his efforts to obtain it by an individual who
was generally considered less deserving of it
than he, my informant has distinct recollections ;
and also remembers that his defeat was occasioned principally through the exertions, in behalf of his opponent, of Colonel William Craw-

ford. This affords a key to the cause of Girty's fiendlike conduct toward the Colonel when, some ten years afterward, the latter was bound to the stake at one of the Wyandot towns, and in the extremity of his agony besought the renegade to put an end to his misery by shooting him through the heart: it offers no apology, however, for Girty's brutality on that occasion.

The career of the renegade, commenced by treason and pursued through blood to the knee, affords a good lesson, which might well receive some remark; but this narrative has already extended to an unexpected length, and must here close. It is a dark record ; but the histories of all new countries contain somewhat similar passages, and their preservation in this form may not be altogether without usefulness.[*]

* Gallagher.

CHAPTER XVIII.

Season of repose—Colonel Boone buys land—Builds a log-house and goes to farming—Kentucky organized on a new basis—The three counties united in one district, and courts established—Colonel Boone surprised by Indians—Escapes by a bold stratagem—Increase of emigration—Transportation of goods commences—Primitive manners and customs of the settlers—Hunting—The autumn hunt—The hunting camp—Qualification of a good hunter—Animals hunted—The process of building and furnishing a cabin—The house-warming.

AFTER the series of Indian hostilities recorded in the chapters immediately preceding this, Kentucky enjoyed a season of comparative repose. The cessation of hostilities between the United States and Great Britain in 1783, and the probable speedy cession of the British posts on the Northwestern frontier, discouraged the Indians, stopped their customary incursions on the Kentuckians, and gave them leisure to acquire and cultivate new tracts of land.

Colonel Boone, notwithstanding the heavy

loss of money (which has been already mentioned) as he was on his journey to North Carolina, was now able to purchase several locations of
land. He had been compensated for his military
services by the Commonwealth of Virginia, to
which Kentucky still belonged. On one of his
locations he built a comfortable log-house and
recommenced farming, with his usual industry
and perseverance, varying the pursuits of agri-
culture with occasional indulgence in his favorite sport of hunting.

In 1783 Kentucky organized herself on a
new basis, Virginia having united three counties
into one district, having a court of common law
and chancery for the whole territory which
now forms the State of Kentucky. The seat of
justice at first was at Harrodsburg; but for
want of convenient accommodations for the
sessions of the courts, they were subsequently
removed to Danville, which, in consequence,
became for a season the center and capital of
the State.*

A singular and highly characteristic adven-

* Perking. Peck.

ture, in which Boone was engaged about this time, is thus narrated by Mr. Peck:

"Though no hostile attacks from Indians disturbed the settlements, still there were small parties discovered or *signs* seen on the frontier settlements. On one occasion about this period four Indians came to the farm of Colonel Boone. and nearly succeeded in taking him prisoner. The particulars are given as they were narrated by Boone himself, at the wedding of a grand-daughter a few months before his decease, and they furnish an illustration of his habitual self-possession and tact with Indians. At a short distance from his cabin he had raised a small patch of tobacco to supply his neighbors (for Boone never used the 'filthy weed' himself), the amount, perhaps, of one hundred and fifty hills.

"As a shelter for curing it, he had built an enclosure of rails, a dozen feet in height, and covered it with cane and grass. Stalks of to-bacco are usually split and strung on sticks about four feet in length. The ends of these are laid on poles, placed across the tobacco house, and in tiers, one above the other to the roof. Boone had fixed his temporary shelter in such a manner as to have three tiers. He had covered the lower tier, and the tobacco had become dry, when he entered the shelter for the purpose of removing the sticks to the upper tier, preparatory to gathering the remainder of the crop. He had hoisted up the sticks from the lower to the second tier and was standing on the poles that supported it while raising the sticks to the upper tier, when four stout Indians with guns entered the low door and called him by name. 'Now, Boone, we got you. You no get away more. We carry you off to Chillicothe this time. You no cheat us any more.' Boone looked down upon their upturned faces, saw their loaded guns pointed at his breast, and recognizing some of his old friends the Shawanees, who had made him prisoner near the Blue Licks in 1778, coolly and pleasantly responded, 'Ah, old friends, glad to see you.' Perceiving that they manifested impatience to have him come down, he told them he was quite willing to go with them, and only begged they would wait where they were, and watch him closely, until he could finish removing his tobacco.

"While parleying with them, inquiring after old acquaintances, and proposing to give them his tobacco when cured, he diverted their attention from his purpose until he had collected together a number of sticks of dry tobacco, and so turned them as to fall between the poles directly in their faces. At the same instant he jumped upon them with as much of the dry tobacco as he could gather in his arms, filling their mouths and eyes with its pungent dust; and blinding and disabling them from following him, rushed out and hastened to his cabin, where he had the means of defense. Notwithstanding the narrow escape, he could not resist the temptation, after retreating some fifteen or twenty yards, to look round and see the success of his achievement. The Indians, blinded and nearly suffocated, were stretching out their hands and feeling about in different directions, calling him by name and cursing him for a rogue, and themselves for fools. The old man, in telling the story, imitated their gestures and tones of voice with great glee."

Emigration to Kentucky was now rapidly on the increase, and many new settlements were formed. The means of establishing comfortable homesteads increased. Horses, cattle, and swine were rapidly increasing in number, and trading in various commodities became more general. From Philadelphia merchandise was transported to Pittsburg on pack-horses, and thence taken down the Ohio River in flat boats and distributed among the settlements on its banks. Country stores, land speculators, and paper money made their appearance affording a clear augury of the future activity of the West in commercial industry and enterprise.

Most of the settlers came from the interior of North Carolina and Virginia; and brought with them the manners and customs of those States These manners and customs were primitive enough. The following exceedingly graphic description, which we transcribe from "Doddridge's Notes," will afford the reader a compe

tent idea of rural life in the times of Daniel
Boone.

"HUNTING.—This was an important part of
the employment of the early settlers of this
country. For some years the woods supplied
them with the greater amount of their subsistence, and with regard to some families, at certain
times, the whole of it ; for it was no uncommon
thing for families to live several months without a mouthful of bread. It frequently happened that there was no breakfast until it was
obtained from the woods. Fur and peltry were
the people's money. They had nothing else to
give in exchange for rifles, salt, and iron, on the
other side of the mountains.

"The fall and early part of the winter was
the season for hunting deer, and the whole of
the winter, including part of the spring, for
bears and fur-skinned animals. It was a customary saying that fur is good during every
month in the name of which the letter B
occurs.

"The class of hunters with whom I was best
acquainted, were those whose hunting ranges

were on the eastern side of the river, and at the
distance of eight or nine miles from it. As soon
as the leaves were pretty well down, and the
weather became rainy, accompanied with light
snows, these men, after acting the part of hus-
bandmen, so far as the state of warfare permitted
them to do so, soon began to feel that they were
hunters. They became uneasy at home. Everything about them became disagreeable. The
house was too warm, the feather-bed too soft,
and even the good wife was not thought, for the
time being, a proper companion. The mind of
the hunter was wholly occupied with the camp
and chase.

"I have often seen them get up early in the
morning at this season, walk hastily out, and
look anxiously to the woods and snuff the autumnal winds with the highest rapture, then re
turn into the house and cast a quick and atten
tive look at the rifle which was always suspended to a joist by a couple of buck horns, or
little forks. His hunting dog, understanding
the intentions of his master, would wag his
tail, and by every blandishment in his power

express his readiness to accompany him to the woods.

"A day was soon appointed for the march of the little cavalcade to the camp. Two or three horses furnished with pack-saddles were loaded with flour, Indian meal, blankets, and every-thing else requisite for the use of the hunter.

"A hunting camp, or what was called a half-faced cabin, was of the following form; the back part of it was sometimes a large log; at the distance of eight or ten feet from this, two stakes were set in the ground a few inches apart, and at the distance of eight or ten feet from these, two more, to receive the ends of the poles for the sides of the camp. The whole slope of the roof, was from the front to the back. The covering was made of slabs, skins, or blankets, or, if in the spring of the year, the bark of hickory or ash trees. The front was entirely open. The fire was built directly before this opening. The cracks between the logs were filled with moss. Dry leaves served for a bed. It is thus that a couple of men in a few hours will construct for themselves a temporary, but tolerably comfortable defense, from the inclemencies of the weather. The beaver, otter, muskrat and squirrel are scarcely their equals in despatch in fabricating for themselves a covert from the tempest!

"A little more pains would have made a hunting camp a defense against the Indians. A cabin ten feet square, bullet proof, and furnished with port-holes would have enabled two or three hunters to hold twenty Indians at bay for any length of time. But this precaution I believe was never attended to; hence the hunters were often surprised and killed in their camps.

"The site for the camp was selected with all the sagacity of the woodsman, so as to have it sheltered by the surrounding hills from every wind, but more especially from those of the north and west.

"An uncle of mine, of the name of Samuel Teter, occupied the same camp for several years in succession. It was situated on one of the southern branches of Cross Creek. Although I lived for many years not more than fifteen miles from the place, it was not till within a very few years ago that I discovered its situation. It was shown me by a gentleman living in the neighborhood. Viewing the hills round about it I soon perceived the sagacity of the hunter in the site for his camp. Not a wind could touch him ; and unless by the report of his gun or the sound of his ax, it would have been by mere accident if an Indian had discovered his concealment.

" Hunting was not a mere ramble in pursuit of game, in which there was nothing of skill and calculation ; on the contrary, the hunter, before he set out in the morning, was informed, by the state of the weather, in what situation he might reasonably expect to meet with his game ; whether on the bottoms, sides or tops of the hills. In stormy weather, the deer always seek the most sheltered places, and the leeward side of the hills. In rainy weather, in which there is not much wind, they keep in the open woods on the highest ground.

" In every situation it was requisite for the hunter to ascertain the course of the wind. so as

to get the leeward of the game. This he effected by putting his finger in his mouth, and
holding it there until it became warm, then
holding it above his head, the side which first
becomes cold shows which way the wind blows.

"As it was requisite too for the hunter to
know the cardinal points, he had only to observe
the trees to ascertain them. The bark of an
aged tree is thicker and much rougher on the
north than on the south side. The same thing
may be said of the moss: it is much thicker and
stronger on the north than on the south side of
the trees.

"The whole business of the hunter consists of
a succession of intrigues. From morning till
night he was on the alert to *gain* the wind of
his game, and approach them without being discovered. If he succeeded in killing a deer, he
skinned it, and hung it up out of the reach of
the wolves, and immediately resumed the chase
till the close of the evening, when he bent his
course toward the camp; when he arrived there
he kindled up his fire, and together with his
fellow hunter, cooked his supper. The supper

finished, the adventures of the day furnished the tales for the evening. The spike buck, the two and three-pronged buck, the doe and barren doe, figured through their anecdotes with great advantage. It should seem that after hunting awhile on the same ground, the hunters became acquainted with nearly all the gangs of deer within their range, so as to know each flock of them when they saw them. Often some old buck, by the means of his superior sagacity and watchfulness, saved his little gang from the hunter's skill, by giving timely notice of his approach. The cunning of the hunter and that of the old buck were staked against each other, and it frequently happened that at the conclusion of the hunting season, the old fellow was left the free uninjured tenant of his forest; but if his rival succeeded in bringing him down, the victory was followed by no small amount of boasting on the part of the conqueror.

"When the weather was not suitable for hunting, the skins and carcasses of the game were brought in and disposed of.

"Many of the hunters rested from their labors

on the Sabbath day; some from a motive of piety; others said that whenever they hunted on Sunday, they were sure to have bad luck on the rest of the week.

"THE HOUSE-WARMING.—I will proceed to state the usual manner of settling a young couple in the world.

"A spot was selected on a piece of land of one of the parents, for their habitation. A day was appointed shortly after their marriage, for commencing the work of building their cabin. The fatigue-party consisted of choppers, whose business it was to fell the trees and cut them off at proper length. A man with a team for haul-ing them to the place and arranging them, prop-erly assorted, at the sides and ends of the building; a carpenter, if such he might be called, whose business it was to search the woods for a proper tree for making clapboards for the roof. The tree for this purpose must be straight-grained, and from three to four feet in diameter. The boards were split four feet long, with a large frow, and as wide as the timber would allow. They were used without planing or shaving. Another division were employed in getting puncheons for the floor of the cabin; this was done by slitting trees, about eighteen inches in diameter, and hewing the faces of them with a broad-ax. They were half the length of the floor they were intended to make. The materials for the cabin were mostly prepared on the first day, and sometimes the foundation laid in the evening. The second day was allotted for the raising.

"In the morning of the next day the neighbors collected for the raising. The first thing to be done was the election of four corner men, whose business it was to notch and place the logs. The rest of the company furnished them with the timbers. In the meantime the boards and puncheons were collecting for the floor and roof, so that by the time the cabin was a few rounds high, the sleepers and floor began to be laid. The door was made by sawing or cutting the logs in one side so as to make an opening about three feet wide. This opening was secured by upright pieces of timber about three inches thick, through which holes were bored into the ends of the logs for the purpose of pinning them fast. A similar opening, but wider, was made at the end for the chimney. This was built of logs, and made large, to admit of a back and jambs of stone. At the square, two end logs projected a foot or eighteen inches beyond the wall, to receive the butting poles, as they were called, against which the ends of the first row of clapboards was supported. The roof was formed by making the end logs shorter, until a single log formed the comb of the roof, on these logs the clapboards were placed, the ranges of them lapping some distance over those next below them, and kept in their places by logs, placed at proper distances upon them.

" The roof, and sometimes the floor, were finished on the same day of the raising. A third day was commonly spent by a few carpenters in leveling off the floor, making a clapboard door and a table. This last was made of a split slab, and supported by four round legs set in auger-holes. Some three-legged stools were made in the same manner. Some pins stuck in the logs at the back of the house supported some clapboards which served for shelves for the table furniture. A single fork, placed with its lower end in a hole in the floor, and the upper end fastened to a joist, served for a bedstead, by placing a pole in the fork with one end through a crack between the logs of the wall. This front pole was crossed by a shorter one within the fork, with its outer end through another crack. From the front pole, through a crack between the logs of the end of the house, the boards were put on which formed the bottom of the bed. Sometimes other poles were pinned to the fork a little distance above these, for the purpose of supporting the front and foot of the bed, while the walls were the supports of its back and head. A few pegs around the walls for a display of the coats of the women and hunting-shirts of the men, and two small forks or buck-horns to a joist for the rifle and shot-pouch, completed the carpenter work.

"In the meantime masons were at work. With the heart pieces of the timber of which the clapboards were made, they made billets for chunking up the cracks between the logs of the cabin and chimney; a large bed of mortar was made for daubing up these cracks; a few stones formed the back and jambs of the chimney.

"The cabin being finished, the ceremony of house-warming took place, before the young couple were permitted to move into it.

" The house-warming was a dance of a whole night's continuance, made up of the relations of the bride and groom and their neighbors. On the day following the young couple took possession of their new mansion."

CHAPTER XIX.

Before leaving the subject of the actual con dition of the early settlers in the West, we take another extract from "Doddridge's Notes," comprising his observations on the state of the mechanic arts among them and an account of some of their favorite sports.

"Mechanic Arts.—In giving the history of the state of the mechanic arts as they were exercised at an early period of the settlement of this country, I shall present a people, driven by necessity to perform works of mechanical skill,

266

far beyond what a person enjoying all the advantages of civilization would expect from a population placed in such destitute circumstances.

"My reader will naturally ask, where were their mills for grinding grain? Where their tanners for making leather? Where their smiths' shops for making and repairing their farming utensils? Who were their carpenters, tailors, cabinet-workmen, shoemakers, and weavers? The answer is those manufacturers did not exist; nor had they any tradesmen, who were professedly such. Every family were under the necessity of doing everything for themselves as well as they could. The hominy block and hand-mills were in use in most of our houses. The first was made of a large block of wood about three feet long, with an excavation burned in one end, wide at the top and narrow at the bottom, so that the action of the pestle on the bottom threw the corn up to the sides toward the top of it, from whence it continually fell down into the center.

"In consequence of this movement, the whole

mass of the grain was pretty equally subjected to the strokes of the pestle. In the fall of the year while the Indian corn was soft, the block and pestle did very well for making meal for johnny-cake and mush; but were rather slow when the corn became hard.

"The sweep was sometimes used to lessen the toil of pounding grain into meal. This was a pole of some springy, elastic wood, thirty feet long or more; the butt end was placed under the side of a house, or a large stump; this pole was supported by two forks, placed about one-third of its length from the butt end, so as to elevate the small end about fifteen feet from the ground; to this was attached, by a large mortise, a piece of sapling about five or six inches in diameter and eight or ten feet long. The lower end of this was shaped so as to answer for a pestle. A pin of wood was put through it, at a proper height, so that two persons could work at the sweep at once. This simple machine very much lessened the labor and expedited the work.

"I remember that when a boy I put up an excellent sweep at my father's. It was made of a sugar-tree sapling. It was kept going almost constantly from morning till night by our neighbors and friends for several weeks.

"In the Greenbriar country, where were a number of saltpeter caves, the first settlers made plenty of excellent gunpowder by the means of those sweeps and mortars.

"A machine, still more simple than the mortar and pestle, was used for making meal while the corn was too soft to be beaten. It was called a grater. This was a half-circular piece of tin, perforated with a punch from the concave side, and nailed by its edges to a block of wood. The ears of corn were rubbed on the rough edge of the holes, while the meal fell through them on the board or block, to which the grater was nailed, which, being in a slanting direction, discharged the meal into a cloth or bowl placed for its reception. This, to be sure, was a slow way of making meal; but necessity has no law.

"The hand-mill was better than the mortar and grater. It was made of two circular stones, the lowest of which was called the bed-stone the upper one the runner. These were placed in a hoop, with a spout for discharging the meal. A staff was let into a hole in the upper surface of the runner, near the outer edge and its upper end through a hole in a board fastened to a joist above, so that two persons could be employed in turning the mill at the same time. The grain was put into the opening in the runner by hand. The mills are still in use in Palestine, the ancient country of the Jews. To a mill of this sort our Saviour alluded when, with reference to the destruction of Jerusalem, he said : 'Two women shall be grinding at a mill, the one shall be taken and the other left.'

"This mill is much preferable to that used at present in upper Egypt for making the dhourra bread. It is a smooth stone, placed on an inclined plane, upon which the grain is spread, which is made into meal by rubbing another stone up and down upon it.

"Our first water mills were of that description denominated tub-mills. It consists of a perpendicular shaft, to the lower end of which an horizontal wheel of about four or five feet in diameter is attached, the upper end passes through the bedstone and carries the runner after the manner of a trundlehead. These mills were built with very little expense, and many of them answered the purpose very well.

"Instead of bolting cloths, sifters were in general use. These were made of deer skins in the state of parchment, stretched over a hoop and perforated with a hot wire.

"Our clothing was all of domestic manufacture. We had no other resource for clothing, and this, indeed, was a poor one. The crops of flax often failed, and the sheep were destroyed by the wolves. Linsey, which is made of flax and wool, the former the chain and the latter the filling, was the warmest and the most substantial cloth we could make. Almost every house contained a loom, and almost every woman was a weaver.

"Every family tanned their own leather. The tan vat was a large trough sunk to the upper edge in the ground. A quantity of bark was easily obtained every spring in clearing and fencing land. This, after drying, was brought in, and in wet days was shaved and pounded on a block of wood with an ax or mallet. Ashes were used in place of lime for taking off the hair. Bears' oil, hogs' lard, and tallow answered the place of fish oil. The leather, to be sure, was coarse; but it was substantially good. The operation of currying was performed by a drawing-knife with its edge turned, after the manner of a currying-knife. The blocking for the leather was made of soot and hog's lard.

"Almost every family contained its own tailors and shoemakers. Those who could not make shoes could make shoepacks. These, like moccasins, were made of a single piece on the top of the foot. This was about two inches broad and circular at the lower end. To this the main piece of leather was sewed, with a gathering stitch. The seam behind was like that of a moccasin. To the shoepack a sole was sometimes added. The women did the tailor-work. They could all cut out, and make hunting shirts, leggins, and drawers.

"The state of society which exists in every

country at an early period of its settlements is well calculated to call into action every native mechanical genius. So it happened in this country. There was in almost every neighbor. hood some one whose natural ingenuity enabled him to do many things for himself and his neighbors, far above what could have been rea. sonably expected. With the few tools which they brought with them into the country, they certainly performed wonders. Their plows, harrows with their wooden teeth, and sleds, were in many instances well made. Their cooper-ware, which comprehended everything for holding milk and water, was generally pretty well executed. The cedar-ware, by hav. ing alternately a white and red stave, was then thought beautiful; many of their puncheon floors were very neat, their joints close, and the top even and smooth. Their looms, although heavy, did very well. These who could not exercise these mechanic arts were under the necessity of giving labor or barter to their neighbors, in ex. change for the use of them, so far as their necessities required.

18

" SPORTS.—One important pastime of our boys was that of imitating the noise of every bird and beast in the woods. This faculty was not merely a pastime, but a very necessary part of education, on account of its utility in certain circumstances. The imitations of the gobbling, and other sounds of wild turkeys, often brought those keen-eyed and ever-watchful tenants of the forests within the reach of their rifle. The bleating of the fawn brought its dam to her death in the same way. The hunter often collected a company of mopish owls to the trees about his camp, and amused himself with their hoarse screaming ; his howl would raise and obtain responses from a pack of wolves, so as to inform him of their neighborhood, as well as guard him against their depredations.

" This imitative faculty was sometimes requisite as a measure of precaution in war. The Indians, when scattered about in a neighborhood, often collected together, by imitating turkeys by day and wolves or owls by night. In similar situations, our people did the same. I have often witnessed the consternation of a whole settlement, in consequence of a few screeches of owls. An early and correct use of this imitative faculty was considered as an indication that its possessor would become, in due time, a good hunter and valiant warrior. Throwing the tomahawk was another boyish sport, in which many acquired considerable skill. The tomahawk, with its handle of a certain length, will make a given number of turns in a given distance. Say in five steps, it will strike with the edge, the handle downward; at the distance of seven and a half, it will strike with the edge, the handle upward, and so on. A little experience enabled the boy to measure the distance with his eye, when walking through the woods, and strike a tree with his tomahawk in any way he chose.

"The athletic sports of running, jumping, and wrestling were the pastimes of boys, in common with the men.

"A well-grown boy, at the age of twelve or thirteen years, was furnished with a small rifle and shot-pouch. He then became a fort soldier, and had his porthole assigned him. Hunting squirrels, turkeys, and raccoons soon made him expert in the use of his gun.

" Dancing was the principal amusement of our young people of both sexes. Their dances, to be sure, were of the simplest form. Three and four-handed reels and jigs. Country dances, cotillions, and minuets were unknown. I remember to have seen, once or twice, a dance which was called " The Irish Trot," but I have long since forgotten its figure.

" Shooting at marks was a common diversion among the men, when their stock of ammunition would allow it ; this, however, was far from being always the case. The present mode of shooting off-hand was not then in practise. This mode was not considered as any trial of the value of a gun, nor, indeed, as much of a test of the skill of a marksman. Their shooting was from a rest, and at as great a distance as the length and weight of the barrel of the gun would throw a ball on a horizontal level. Such was their regard to accuracy, in those sportive trials of their rifles. and of their own skill in the use of them, that they often put moss, or some other soft substance on the log or stump from which they shot, for fear of having the bullet thrown from the mark by the spring of the barrel. When the rifle was held to the side of a tree for a rest, it was pressed against it as lightly as possible, for the same reason.

" Rifles of former times were different from those of modern date ; few of them carried more than forty-five bullets to the pound. Bullets of a less size were not thought sufficiently heavy for hunting or war."

Our readers will pardon the length of these extracts from Doddridge, as they convey accurate pictures of many scenes of Western life in the times of Daniel Boone. We add to them a single extract from "Ramsay's Annals of Tennessee." The early settlement of that State took place about the same time with that of Kentucky, and was made by emigrants from the same region. The following remarks are therefore perfectly applicable to the pioneers of Kentucky.

" The settlement of Tennessee was unlike that of the present new country of the United States. Emigrants from the Atlantic cities, and from most points in the Western interior, now embark upon steamboats or other craft, and carrying with them all the conveniences and comforts of civilized life—indeed, many of its luxuries—are, in a few days, without toil, danger, or exposure, transported to their new abodes, and in a few months are surrounded with the appendages of home, of civilization, and the blessings of law and of society. The wilds of Minnesota and Nebraska by the agency of steam, or the stalwart arms of Western boatmen, are at once transformed into the settlements of a commercial and civilized people. Independence and St. Paul, six months after they are laid off, have their stores and their workshops, their artisans, and their mechanics. The mantua-maker and the tailor arrive in the same boat with the carpenter and mason. The professional man and the printer quickly follow. In the succeeding year the piano, the drawing-room, the restaurant, the billiard table, the church bell, the village and the city in miniature, are all found, while the neighboring interior is yet a wilderness and a desert. The town and comfort. taste and urbanity are first ; the clearing, the farm-house, the wagon road and the improved country, second. It was far different on the frontier in Tennessee. At first a single Indian trail was the only entrance to the eastern border of it, and for many years admitted only of the hunter and the pack-horse. It was not till the year 1776 that a wagon was seen in Tennessee. In consequence of the want of roads—as well as of the great distance from sources of supply—the first inhabitants were without tools, and, of course, without mechanics—much more, without the conveniences of living and the comforts of housekeeping. Luxuries were absolutely unknown. Salt was brought on pack-horses from Augusta and Richmond, and readily commanded ten dollars a bushel. The salt gourd, in every cabin, was considered as a treasure. The sugar maple furnished the only article of luxury on the frontier; coffee and tea being unknown, or beyond the reach of the settlers ; sugar was seldom made, and was only used for the sick, or in the preparation of a *sweetened dram* at a wedding, or the arrival of a newcomer. The appendages of the kitchen, the cupboard, and the table were scanty and simple.

" Iron was brought at great expense, from the forges east of the mountain, on pack horses, and was sold at an enormous price. Its use was, for this reason, confined to the construction and repair of plows and other farming utensils. Hinges, nails, and fastenings of that material were seldom seen.

" The costume of the first settlers corresponded well with the style of their buildings and the quality of their furniture. The hunting-shirt of the militiaman and the hunter was in general use. The rest of their apparel was in keeping with it—plain, substantial, and well adapted for comfort, use, and economy. The apparel of the pioneer's family was all home-made, and in a whole neighborhood there would not be seen, at the first settlement of the country, a single article of dress of foreign growth or manufacture. Half the year, in many families, shoes were not worn. Boots, a fur hat, and a coat with buttons on each side attracted the gaze of the beholder and sometimes received censure and rebuke. A

stranger from the old States chose to doff his
ruffles, his broadcloth, and his queue, rather
than endure the scoff and ridicule of the backwoodsmen.

"The dwelling-house, on every frontier in
Tennessee, was the log-cabin. A carpenter and
a mason were not needed to build them—much
less the painter, the glazier, or the upholsterer.
Every settler had, besides his rifle, no other instrument but an ax, a hatchet, and a butcher
knife. A saw, an auger, a froe, and a broad-
ax would supply a whole settlement, and were
used as common property in the erection of the
log-cabin. The floor of the cabin was sometimes the earth. No saw-mill was yet erected ;
and, if the means or leisure of the occupant
authorized it, he split out puncheons for the floor
and for the shutter of the entrance to his cabin.
The door was hung with wooden hinges and
fastened by a wooden latch.

"Such was the habitation of the pioneer Ten-
nessean. Scarcely can one of these structures,
venerable for their years and the associations
which cluster around them, be now seen in Ten-

nessee. Time and improvement have displaced them. Here and there in the older counties, may yet be seen the old log-house, which sixty years ago sheltered the first emigrant, or gave, for the time, protection to a neighborhood assembled within its strong and bullet-proof walls. Such an one is the east end of Mr. Martin's house, at Campbell's Station, and the center part of the mansion of this writer, at Mecklenburg, once Gilliam's Station, changed somewhat, it is true, in some of its aspects, but preserving even yet, in the height of the story and in its old-fashioned and capacious fireplace, some of the features of primitive architecture on the frontier. Such, too, is the present dwelling-house of Mr. Tipton, on Ellejoy, in Blount County, and that of Mr. Glasgow Snoddy, in Sevier County. But these old buildings are becoming exceedingly rare, and soon not one of them will be seen. Their unsightly proportions and rude architecture will not much longer offend modern taste, nor provoke the idle and irreverent sneer of the fastidious and the fashionable. When the last one of these pioneer houses shall have fallen into decay and ruins, the memory of their first occupants will still be immortal and indestructible.

" The interior of the cabin was no less unpretending and simple. The whole furniture, of the one apartment—answering in these primitive times the purposes of the kitchen, the dining-room, the nursery and the dormitory—were a plain home-made bedstead or two, some split-bottomed chairs and stools ; a large puncheon, supported on four legs, used, as occasion required, for a bench or a table, a water shelf and a bucket ; a spinning-wheel, and sometimes a loom, finished the catalogue. The wardrobe of the family was equally plain and simple. The walls of the house were hung round with the dresses of the females, the hunting-shirts, clothes, and the arms and shot-pouches of the men.

" The labor and employment of a pioneer family were distributed in accordance with surrounding circumstances. To the men was assigned the duty of procuring subsistence and materials for clothing, erecting the cabin and the station, opening and cultivating the farm, hunting the wild beasts, and repelling and pursuing the Indians. The women spun the flax, the cotton and wool, wove the cloth, made them up, milked, churned, and prepared the food, and did their full share of the duties of housekeeping. Another thus describes them : " There we behold woman in her true glory ; not a doll to carry silks and jewels, not a puppet to be dandled by fops, an idol of profane adoration, reverenced to-day, discarded to-morrow ; admired, but not respected ; desired, but not esteemed ; ruling by passion, not affection ; imparting her weakness, not her constancy, to the sex she should exalt ; the source and mirror of vanity. We see her as a wife, partaking of the cares, and guiding the labors of her husband, and by her domestic diligence spreading cheerfulness all around ; for his sake, sharing the decent refinements of the world, without being fond of them ; placing all her joy, all her happiness in the merited approbation of the man she loves. As a mother, we find her the affectionate, the ardent instructress of the children she has reared from infancy and trained them up to thought and virtue, to meditation and benevolence : address

ing them as rational beings, and preparing them
to become men and women in their turn.

"'Could there be happiness or comfort in
such dwellings and such a state of society? To
those who are accustomed to modern refinements, the truth appears like fable. The early
occupants of log-cabins were among the most
happy of mankind. Exercise and excitement
gave them health; they were practically equal;
common danger made them mutually depend-
ent; brilliant hopes of future wealth and distinction led them on; and as there was ample
room for all, and as each newcomer increased
individual and general security, there was little
room for that envy, jealousy, and hatred which
constitute a large portion of human misery in
older societies. Never were the story, the joke
the song, and the laugh better enjoyed than
upon the hewed blocks, or puncheon stools
around the roaring log fire of the early Western
settler. The lyre of Apollo was not hailed
with more delight in primitive Greece than the
advent of the first fiddler among the dwellers
of the wilderness; and the polished daughters

of the East never enjoyed themselves half so well, moving to the music of a full band, upon the elastic floor of their ornamented ball-room, as did the daughters of the emigrants, keeping time to a self-taught fiddler, on the bare earth or puncheon floor of the primitive log cabin. The smile of the polished beauty is the wave of the lake, where the breeze plays gently over it, and her movement is the gentle stream which drains it; but the laugh of the log-cabin is the gush of nature's fountain, and its movement, its leaping water.' *

"On the frontier the diet was necessarily plain and homely, but exceedingly abundant and nutritive. The Goshen of America † furnished the richest milk, the finest butter, and the most savory and delicious meats. In their rude cabins, with their scanty and inartificial furniture, no people ever enjoyed in wholesome food a greater variety, or a superior quality of the necessaries of life. For bread, the Indian corn was exclusively used. It was not till 1790 that the settlers on the rich bottoms of Cumberland

* Kendall.   † Butler.

and Nollichucky discovered the remarkable ad·
aptation of the soil and climate of Tennessee to
the production of this grain. Emigrants from
James River, the Catawba, and the Santee were
surprised at the amount and quality of the corn
crops, surpassing greatly the best results of agri·
cultural labor and care in the Atlantic States.
This superiority still exists, and Tennessee, by the
census of 1850, was *the* corn State. Of all the
farinacea corn is best adapted to the condition
of a pioneer people ; and if idolatry is at all
justifiable, Ceres, or certainly the Goddess of
Indian corn, should have had a temple and
worshipers among the pioneers of Tennessee.
Without that grain, the frontier settlements
could not have been formed and maintained.
It is the most certain crop—requires the least
preparation of the ground—is most congenial to
a virgin soil—needs not only the least amount
of labor in its culture, but comes to maturity in
the shortest time. The pith of the matured
stalk of the corn is esculent and nutritious ; and
the stalk itself, compressed between rollers,
furnishes what is known as corn-stalk molasses.

"This grain requires, also, the least care and trouble in preserving it. It may safely stand all winter upon the stalk without injury from the weather or apprehension of damage by disease, or the accidents to which other grains are subject. Neither smut nor rust, nor weavil nor snow-storm, will hurt it. After its maturity, it is also prepared for use or the granary with little labor. The husking is a short process, and is even advantageously delayed till the moment arrives for using the corn. The machinery for converting it into food is also exceedingly simple and cheap. As soon as the ear is fully formed, it may be roasted or boiled, and forms thus an excellent and nourishing diet. At a later period it may be grated, and furnishes, in this form, the sweetest bread. The grains boiled in a variety of modes, either whole or broken in a mortar, or roasted in the ashes, or popped in an oven, are well relished. If the grain is to be converted into meal, a simple tub-mill answers the purpose best, as the meal *least perfectly ground* is always preferred. A bolting-cloth is not needed, as it diminishes the sweetness and value of the flour. The catalogue of the advantages of this meal might be extended further. Boiled in water, it forms the frontier dish called *mush*, which was eaten with milk, with honey, molasses, butter or gravy. Mixed with cold water, it is at once ready for the cook; covered with hot ashes, the preparation is called the ash cake; placed upon a piece of clapboard, and set near the coals, it forms the journey-cake; or managed in the same way, upon a helveless hoe, it forms the hoe-cake; put in an oven, and covered over with a heated lid, it is called, if in a large mass, a pone or loaf; if in smaller quantities, dodgers. It has the further advantage, over all other flour, that it requires in its preparation few culinary utensils, and neither sugar, yeast, eggs, spices, soda, potash, or other *et ceteras*, to qualify or perfect the bread. To all this it may be added, that it is not only cheap and well tasted, but it is unquestionably the most wholesome and nutritive food. The largest and healthiest people in the world have lived upon it exclusively. It formed the principal bread of that robust race of men—giants in miniature—which, half a century since, was seen on the frontier.

"The dignity of history is not lowered by this enumeration of the pre-eminent qualities of Indian corn. The rifle and the ax have had their influence in subduing the wilderness to the purposes of civilization, and they deserve their eulogists and trumpeters. Let pæans be sung all over the mighty West to Indian corn—without it, the West would have still been a wilderness. Was the frontier suddenly invaded? Without commissary or quartermaster, or other sources of supply, each soldier parched a peck of corn; a portion of it was put into his pockets, the remainder in his wallet, and, throwing it upon his saddle, with his rifle on his shoulder, he was ready, in half an hour, for the campaign. Did a flood of emigration inundate the frontier with an amount of consumers disproportioned to the supply of grain? The facility of raising the Indian corn, and its early maturity, gave promise and guaranty that the scarcity would be temporary and tolerable. Did the safety of the frontier demand the services of every adult militiaman? The boys and women could, themselves, raise corn and furnish ample supplies of bread. The crop could be gathered next year. Did an autumnal intermittent confine the whole family or the entire population to the sick-bed? This certain concomitant of the clearing, and cultivating the new soil, mercifully withholds its paroxysms till the crop of corn is made. It requires no further labor or care afterward. Pæans, say we, and a temple and worshipers, to the Creator of Indian corn! The frontier man could gratefully say: 'He maketh me to lie down in green pastures. He leadeth me beside the still waters. Thou *preparest a table before me in presence of mine enemies.*'

"The sports of the frontier men were mainly athletic, or warlike—the chase, the bear hunt, the deer drive, shooting at the target, throwing the tomahawk, jumping, boxing and wrestling, foot and horse-racing. Playing marbles and pitching dollars, cards and backgammon were little known, and were considered base or effeminate. The bugle, the violin, the fife and drum, furnished all the musical entertainments. These, were much used and passionately admired. Weddings, military trainings, house-raisings, chopping frolics, were often followed with the fiddle, and dancing, and rural sports."

CHAPTER XX.

KENTUCKY was not yet entirely freed from Indian hostilities. There was no formidable invasion, such as to call for the exertions of Boone, Kenton and the other warriors of the border, but there were several occurrences which occasioned considerable alarm.

293

In the spring of 1784 a number of families started down the Ohio from Louisville in two flat boats. They were pursued by Indians in canoes, but awed by the determined aspect of the whites they drew off, without so much as a gun being fired on either side.

This same spring a party of southern Indians stole some horses from Lincoln County. Three young men, Davis, Caffree and McClure, pursued them, but failing to overtake them, concluded to make reprisals on the nearest Indian settlement. Not far from the Tennessee River, they fell in with an equal number of Indians. The two parties saluted each other in a very friendly manner, and agreed to journey in company. The whites, however, were by no means convinced of the sincerity of their companions, and, seeing them talking together very earnestly, became assured of their hostile intentions. It being determined to anticipate the Indians' attack, Caffree undertook to capture one of them, while his companions shot the other two. Accordingly he sprung upon the nearest Indian, and bore him to the ground; Davis' gun missed fire

but McClure shot his man dead. The remaining Indian sprung to a tree from which shelter
he shot Caffree, who was still struggling with
the Indian he had grappled. He in his turn
was immediately shot by McClure. The Indian
whom Caffree had attacked, extricated himself
from the grasp of his dying antagonist, and
seizing his rifle presented it at Davis, who was
coming to the assistance of his friend. Davis
took to flight, his rifle not being in good order,
and was pursued by the Indian into the wood.
McClure, loading his gun, followed them, but
lost sight of both. Davis was never heard of
afterward.

McClure now concluded to retreat, but he had
not proceeded far, before he met an Indian on
horseback attended by a boy on foot. The
warrior dismounted, and seating himself on a log,
offered his pipe to McClure. Soon other Indians
were seen advancing in the distance, when Mc-
Clure's sociable friend informed him that when
his companions came up they would take him
(McClure) and put him on a horse, tying his
feet under its belly. In order to convey to his

white brother an adequate idea of the honor intended him, the Indian got astride the log and
locked his feet together. McClure took this
opportunity of shooting his amiable but rather
eccentric companion, and then ran off into the
woods and escaped.

This affair, the reader will bear in mind, was
with southern Indians, not with those of the
northwestern tribes, from whom the Kentuckians had suffered most. The only demonstration of hostility made by these, this year, appears
to have been the pursuit of the boats mentioned
before. In March, 1785, a man of the name of
Elliot, who had emigrated to the country near
the mouth of the Kentucky River, was killed
by Indians and his house destroyed and family
dispersed.

As Colonel Thomas Marshall from Virginia
was descending the Ohio, in a flat boat, he was
hailed from the northern shore by a man, who
announced himself as James Girty, and said that
he had been placed by his brother Simon, to
warn all boats of the danger of being attacked
by the Indians. He told them that efforts

would be made to decoy them ashore by means of renegade white men, who would represent themselves as in great distress. He exhorted them to steel their hearts against all such appeals, and to keep the middle of the river. He said that his brother regretted the injuries he had inflicted upon the whites, and would gladly repair them as much as possible, to be re-admitted to their society, having lost all his influence among the Indians. This repentance on the part of Girty seems to have been of short duration, as he remained among the Indians till his death, which according to some took place at the battle of the Thames, though others deny it.

However sincere or lasting Girty's repentance had been, he could never have lived in safety among the whites; he had been too active, and if common accounts are to be credited, too savage in his hostility to them, to admit of forgiveness; and it is probable that a knowledge of this prevented him from abandoning the Indians.

" About the same time," says McClung, " Captain James Ward, at present a highly-respect able citizen of Mason County, Kentucky, was descending the Ohio, under circumstances which rendered a rencontre with the Indians peculiarly to be dreaded. He, together with half a dozen others, one of them his nephew, embarked in a crazy boat, about forty-five feet long and eight feet wide, with no other bulwark than a single pine plank above each gunnel. The boat was much encumbered with baggage, and seven horses were on board. Having seen no enemy for several days, they had become secure and careless, and permitted the boat to drift within fifty yards of the Ohio shore. Suddenly, several hundred Indians showed themselves on the bank, and running down boldly to the water's edge, opened a heavy fire upon the boat. The aston-ishment of the crew may be conceived.

"Captain Ward and his nephew were at the oars when the enemy appeared, and the Captain knowing that their safety depended upon their agility to regain the middle of the river, kept his seat firmly, and exerted his utmost powers at the oar, but his nephew started up at sight of the enemy, seized his rifle, and was in the act of leveling it, when he received a ball in the breast, and fell dead in the bottom of the boat. Unfortunately, his oar fell into the river, and the Captain, having no one to pull against him, rather urged the boat nearer to the hostile shore than otherwise. He quickly seized a plank, however, and giving his oar to another of the crew, he took the station which his nephew had held, and unhurt by the shower of bullets which flew around him, continued to exert himself until the boat had reached a more respectable distance. He then, for the first time, looked around him in order to observe the condition of the crew.

"His nephew lay in his blood, perfectly life-less; the horses had been all killed or mortally wounded. Some had fallen overboard; others were struggling violently and causing their frail bark to dip water so abundantly as to excite the most serious apprehensions. But the crew presented the most singular spectacle. A captain, who had served with reputation in the continental army, seemed now totally bereft of his faculties. He lay upon his back in the bottom of the boat, with hands uplifted, and a countenance in which terror was personified, exclaiming in a tone of despair, "Oh Lord! Oh Lord!" A Dutchman, whose weight might amount to about three hundred pounds, was anxiously engaged in endeavoring to find shelter for his bulky person, which, from the lowness of the gunnels, was a very difficult undertaking. In spite of his utmost efforts, a portion of his posterior luxuriance appeared above the gunnel, and afforded a mark to the enemy, which brought a constant shower of balls around it.

"In vain he shifted his position. The hump still appeared, and the balls still flew around it, until the Dutchman, losing all patience, raised his head above the gunnel, and in a tone of querulous remonstrance, called out, "Oh now! quit tat tamned nonsense, tere, will you!" Not a shot was fired from the boat. At one time, after they had partly regained the current, Captain Ward attempted to bring his rifle to bear upon them, but so violent was the agitation of the boat, from the furious struggles of the horses, that he could not steady his piece within twenty yards of the enemy, and quickly laying it aside, returned to the oar. The Indians followed them down the river for more than an hour, but having no canoes they did not attempt to board; and as the boat was at length transferred to the opposite side of the river, they at length abandoned the pursuit and disappeared. None of the crew, save the young man already mentioned, were hurt, although the Dutchman's seat of honor served as a target for the space of an hour; and the continental captain was deeply mortified at the sudden and, as he said, 'unaccountable' panic which had seized him. Captain Ward himself was protected by a post, which had been fastened to the gunnel, and behind which he sat while rowing." *

"In October, a party of emigrants were attacked near Scaggs' Creek, and six killed. Mrs. McClure, with four children, ran into the woods, where she might have remained concealed, if it had not been for the cries of her infant, whom she could not make up her mind to abandon. The Indians, guided to her hiding

* McClung.

place by these cries, cruelly tomahawked the three oldest children, but made her prisoner with her remaining child. Captain Whitley, with twenty-one men, intercepted the party on its return, and dispersed them, killing two and wounding the same number. The prisoners were rescued. A few days after, another party of emigrants were attacked, and nine of them killed. Captain Whitley again pursued the Indians. On coming up with them, they took to flight. Three were killed in the course of the pursuit; two by the gallant Captain himself. Some other depredations were committed this year, but none of as much importance as those we have mentioned."

These acts of hostility on the part of the Indians led to the adoption of measures for the defense of the Colony, to which we shall presently call the reader's attention.

"Although," says Perkins,* "Kentucky grew rapidly during the year 1784, the emigrants numbering twelve, and the whole population thirty thousand; although a friendly meeting

* "Western Annals."

was held by Thomas J. Dalton, with the Pian-
keshaws, at Vincennes, in April; and though
trade was extending itself into the clearings and
among the canebrakes—Daniel Brodhead having opened his store at Louisville the previous
year and James Wilkinson having come to Lexington in February, as the leader of a large
commercial company, formed in Philadelphia,
still the cool and sagacious mind of Logan led
him to prepare his fellow-citizens for trial and
hardships. He called in the autumn of 1784 a
meeting of the people at Danville, to take measures for defending the country, and at this meeting the whole subject of the position and danger of Kentucky was examined and discussed,
and it was agreed that a convention should
meet in December to adopt some measures for
the security of the settlements in the wilderness.
Upon the 27th of that month it met, nor was it
long before the idea became prominent that Kentucky must ask to be severed from Virginia, and
left to her own guidance and control. But as
no such conception was general, when the delegates to this first convention were chosen, they

deemed it best to appoint a second, to meet during the next May, at which was specially to be considered the topic most interesting to those who were called on to think and vote—a complete separation from the parent State—political independence.

"Several other conventions took place, in which the subject of a separation from Virginia was considered. In 1786 the Legislature of Virginia enacted the necessary preliminary provisions for the separation and erection of Kentucky into an independent State, with the condition that Congress should receive it into the Union, which was finally effected in the year 1792.

" Previously to this event, Indian hostilities were again renewed.

"A number of Indians in April, 1786, stole some horses from the Bear Grass settlement, with which they crossed the Ohio. Colonel Christian pursued them into the Indian country, and, coming up with them, destroyed the whole party. How many there were is not stated. The whites lost two men, one of whom was the Colonel himself, whose death was a severe loss to Kentucky. The following affair, which took place the same year, is given in the language of one who participated in it:

"'After the battle of the Blue Licks, and in 1786, our family removed to Higgins' block house on Licking River, one and a half miles above Cynthiana. Between those periods my father had been shot by the Indians, and my mother married Samuel Van Hook, who had been one of the party engaged in the defense at Ruddell's Station in 1780, and on its surrender was carried with the rest of the prisoners to Detroit.

"'Higgins' Fort, or block-house, had been built at the bank of the Licking, on precipitous rocks, at least thirty feet high, which served to protect us on every side but one. On the morning of the 12th of June, at daylight, the fort, which consisted of six or seven houses, was attacked by a party of Indians, fifteen or twenty in number. There was a cabin outside, below the fort, where William McCombs resided, although absent at that time. His son Andrew, and a man hired in the family, named Joseph

McFall, on making their appearance at the door
to wash themselves, were both shot down—Mc
Combs through the knee, and McFall in the pit
of the stomach. McFall ran to the block-house,
and McCombs fell, unable to support himself
longer, just after opening the door of his cabin,
and was dragged in by his sisters, who barri-
caded the door instantly. On the level and
only accessible side there was a corn field, and
the season being favorable, and the soil rich as
well as new, the corn was more than breast
high. Here the main body of the Indians lay
concealed, while three or four who made the
attack attempted thereby to decoy the whites
outside of the defenses. Failing in this, they
set fire to an old fence and corn-crib, and two
stables, both long enough built to be thoroughly
combustible. These had previously protected
their approach in that direction. Captain Asa
Reese was in command of our little fort.
"Boys," said he, "some of you must run over to
Hinkston's or Harrison's." These were one and
a half and two miles off, but in different directions. Every man declined. I objected, al-

leging as my reason that he would give up the fort before I could bring relief ; but on his assurance that he would hold out, I agreed to go. I jumped off the bank through the thicket of trees, which broke my fall, while they scratched my face and limbs. I got to the ground with a limb clenched in my hands, which I had grasped unawares in getting through. I recovered from the jar in less than a minute, crossed the Licking, and ran up a cow-path on the opposite side, which the cows from one of those forts had beat down in their visits for water. As soon as I had gained the bank I shouted to assure my friends of my safety, and to discourage the enemy. In less than an hour I was back, with a relief of ten horsemen, well armed, and driving in full chase after the Indians. But they had decamped immediately upon hearing my signal, well knowing what it meant, and it was deemed imprudent to pursue them with so weak a party—the whole force in Higgins' block-house hardly sufficing to guard the women and children there. McFall, from whom the bullet could not be extracted, lingered two days and nights in great pain, when he died, as did McCombs, on the ninth day, mortification then taking place.'

"While these depredations were going on, most of the Northwestern tribes were ostensibly at peace with the country, treaties having recently been made. But the Kentuckians, exasperated by the repeated outrages, determined to have resort to their favorite expedient of invading the Indian country. How far they were justified in holding the tribes responsible for the actions of these roving plunderers, the reader must judge for himself. We may remark, however, that it does not seem distinctly proved that the Indians engaged in these attacks belonged to any of the tribes against whom the attack was to be made. But the backwoodsmen were never very scrupulous in such matters. They generally regarded the Indian race as a unit: an offense committed by one warrior might be lawfully punished on another. We often, in reading the history of the West, read of persons who having lost relations by Indians of one tribe, made a practise of killing all whom they met, whether in peace or war. It is evident, as Marshall says, that no authority but that of Congress could render an expedition of this kind lawful. The Governor of Virginia had given instructions to the commanders of the countries to take the necessary means for defense; and the Kentuckians, giving a free interpretation to these instructions, decided that the expedition was necessary and resolved to undertake it.

"General Clark was selected to command it, and to the standard of this favorite officer volunteers eagerly thronged. A thousand men were collected at the Falls of the Ohio, from whence the troops marched by land to St. Vincennes, while the provisions and other supplies were conveyed by water. The troops soon became discouraged. When the provisions reached Vincennes, after a delay of several days on account of the low water, it was found that a large proportion of them were spoiled. In consequence of this, the men were placed upon short allowance, with which, of course, they were not well pleased. In the delay in waiting for the boats, much of the enthusiasm of the men had evaporated; and it is said by some that General Clark despatched a messenger to the towns, in advance of the troops, to offer them the choice of peace or war, which greatly lessened the chances of the success of the expedition. Though this measure would be only complying with the requirements of good faith, it is very doubtful if it was adopted, so utterly at variance would it be with the usual manner of conducting these expeditions.

"At any rate, when the army arrived within two days' march of the Indian towns, no less than three hundred of the men refused to proceed, nor could all the appeals of Clark induce them to alter their determination. They marched off in a body; and so discouraged were the others by this desertion, and the un-favorable circumstances in which they were placed, that a council held the evening after their departure concluded to relinquish the undertaking."

The whole of the troops returned to Kentucky in a very disorderly manner. Thus did this expedition, begun under the most favorable auspices—for the commander's reputation was greater than any other in the West, and the men were the elite of Kentucky—altogether fail of its object, the men not having even seen the enemy. Marshall, in accounting for this unexpected termination, says that Clark was no longer the man he had been; that he had injured his intellect by the use of spirituous liquors. Colonel Logan had at first accompanied Clark, but he soon returned to Kentucky to organize another expedition; that might, while the attention of the Indians was altogether engrossed by the advance of Clark, fall upon some unguarded point. He raised the requisite number of troops without difficulty, and by a rapid march completely surprised one of the Shawanee towns, which he destroyed, killing several of the warriors, and bringing away a number of prisoners. In regard to the results of the measures adopted by the Kentuckians, we quote from Marshall:

"In October of this year, a large number of families traveling by land to Kentucky, known by the name of McNitt's company, were surprised in camp, at night, by a party of Indians between Big and Little Laurel River, and totally defeated, with the loss of twenty-one persons killed; the rest dispersed, or taken prisoners.

"About the same time, Captain Hardin, from the south-western part of the district, with a party of men, made an excursion into the Indian country, surrounding the Saline; he fell in with a camp of Indians whom he attacked and defeated, killing four of them, without loss on his part.

"Some time in December, Hargrove and others were defeated at the mouth of Buck Creek, on the Cumberland River. The Indians attacked in the night, killed one man, and wounded Hargrove; who directly became engaged in a rencontre with an Indian, armed with his tomahawk; of this he was disarmed, but escaped, leaving the weapon with Hargrove, who bore it off, glad to extricate himself. In this year also, Benjamin Price was killed near the three forks of Kentucky.

"Thus ended, in a full renewal of the war, the year whose beginning had happily witnessed the completion of the treaties of peace.

" By this time, one thing must have been obvious to those who had attended to the course of events—and that was, that if the Indians came into the country, whether for peace or war, hostilities were inevitable.

" If the white people went into their country, the same consequences followed. The parties were yet highly exasperated against each other; they had not cooled since the peace, if peace it could be called; and meet where they would, bloodshed was the result.

" Whether the Indians to the north and west had ascertained, or not, that the two ex-peditions of this year were with or without the consent of Congress, they could but think the treaties vain things; and either made by those who had no right to make them, or no power to enforce them. With Kentuckians, it was known that the latter was the fact. To the Indians, the consequence was the same. They knew to a certainty, that the British had not surrendered the posts on the lakes—that it was from them they received their supplies; that they had been deceived, as to the United States

getting the posts, and they were easily per-
suaded to believe, that these posts would not
be transferred; and that in truth, the British,
not the United States, had been the conquerors
in the late war.

"Such were the reflections which the state
of facts would have justified, and at the same
time have disposed them for war. The invasion of their country by two powerful armies
from Kentucky, could leave no doubt of a disposition equally hostile on her part. Congress,
utterly destitute of the means for enforcing the
treaties, either on the one side or the other,
stood aloof, ruminating on the inexhaustible
abundance of her own want of resources—and
the abuse of herself for not possessing them."

After this year, we hear of but few independent expeditions from Kentucky. Their militia
were often called out to operate with the United
States troops, and in Wayne's campaign were of
much service; but this belongs to the general
history of the United States. All that we have
to relate of Kentucky now is a series of preda-
tory attacks by the Indians, varied occasionally

by a spirited reprisal by a small party of whites. It is estimated that fifteen hundred persons were either killed or made prisoners in Kentucky after the year 1783.

" On the night of the 11th of April, 1787,' says McClung, " the house of a widow, in Bourbon County, became the scene of an adventure which we think deserves to be related. She occupied what is generally called a double cabin, in a lonely part of the country, one room of which was tenanted by the old lady herself, together with two grown sons and a widowed daughter, at that time suckling an infant, while the other was occupied by two unmarried daughters, from sixteen to twenty years of age, together with a little girl not more than half grown   The hour was eleven o'clock at night. One of the unmarried daughters was still busily engaged at the loom, but the other members of the family, with the exception of one of the sons, had retired to rest.   Some symptoms of an alarming nature had engaged the attention of the young man for an hour before anything of a decided character took place.

" The cry of owls was heard in the adjoining wood, answering each other in rather an un-usual manner. The horses, which were enclosed as usual in a pound near the house, were more than commonly excited, and by repeated snort-ing and galloping announced the presence of some object of terror. The young man was often upon the point of awakening his brother, but was as often restrained by the fear of incurring ridicule and the reproach of timidity, at that time an unpardonable blemish in the character of a Kentuckian. At length hasty steps were heard in the yard, and quickly afterward sev-eral loud knocks at the door, accompanied by the usual exclamation, 'Who keeps house?' in very good English. The young man, suppos-ing from the language that some benighted settlers were at the door, hastily arose, and was advancing to withdraw the bar which secured it, when his mother, who had long lived upon the frontiers, and had probably detected the Indian tone in the demand for admission, instantly sprung out of bed, and ordered her son not to admit them, declaring that they were Indians.

"She instantly awakened her other son, and the two young men seized their guns, which were always charged, prepared to repel the enemy. The Indians, finding it impossible to enter under their assumed characters, began to thunder at the door with great violence, but a single shot from a loop-hole compelled them to shift the attack to some less exposed point, and, unfortunately, they discovered the door of the other cabin, containing the three daughters. The rifles of the brothers could not be brought to bear upon this point, and by means of several rails taken from the yard fence, the door was forced from its hinges, and the three girls were at the mercy of the savages. One was instantly secured, but the eldest defended herself desperately with a knife which she had been using at the loom, and stabbed one of the Indians to the heart before she was tomahawked.

"In the meantime the little girl, who had been overlooked by the enemy in their eager-ness to secure the others, ran out into the yard, and might have effected her escape, had she taken advantage of the darkness and fled; but instead of that, the terrified little creature ran around the house wringing her hands, and crying out that her sisters were killed. The brothers, unable to hear her cries without risking everything for her rescue, rushed to the door and were preparing to sally out to her assistance, when their mother threw herself before them and calmly declared that the child must be abandoned to its fate; that the sally would sacrifice the lives of all the rest, without the slightest benefit to the little girl. Just then the child uttered a loud scream, followed by a few faint moans, and all was again silent. Presently the crackling of flames was heard, accompanied by a triumphant yell from the Indians, announcing that they had set fire to that division of the house which had been occupied by the daughters, and of which they held undisputed possession.

" The fire was quickly communicated to the rest of the building, and it became necessary to abandon it or perish in the flames. In the one case there was a possibility that some might escape; in the other, their fate would be equally certain and terrible. The rapid approach of the flames cut short their momentary suspense. The door was thrown open, and the old lady, supported by her eldest son, attempted to cross the fence at one point, while her daughter, car· rying her child in her arms, and attended by the younger of the brothers, ran in a different direction. The blazing roof shed a light over the yard but little inferior to that of day, and the savages were distinctly seen awaiting the approach of their victims. The old lady was permitted to reach the stile unmolested, but in the act of crossing received several balls in her breast and fell dead. Her son, providentially, remained unhurt, and by extraordinary agility effected his escape.

"The other party succeeded also in reaching the fence unhurt, but in the act of crossing were vigorously assailed by several Indians, who, throwing down their guns, rushed upon them with their tomahawks. The young man de· fended his sister gallantly, firing upon the enemy as they approached, and then wielding the butt of his rifle with a fury that drew their whole attention upon himself, he gave his sister an opportunity of effecting her escape. He quickly fell, however, under the tomahawks of his enemies, and was found at daylight, scalped and mangled in a shocking manner. Of the whole family consisting of eight persons, when the attack commenced, only three escaped. Four were killed upon the spot, and one (the second daughter) carried off as a prisoner.

"The neighborhood was quickly alarmed, and by daylight about thirty men were assembled under the command of Colonel Edwards. A light snow had fallen during the latter part of the night, and the Indian trail could be pursued at a gallop. It led directly into the mountainous country bordering upon Licking, and afforded evidences of great hurry and precipitation on the part of the fugitives. Unfortunately a hound had been permitted to accompany the whites, and as the trail became fresh and the scent warm, she followed it with eagerness, baying loudly and giving the alarm to the Indians. The consequences of this imprudence were soon displayed. The enemy finding the pursuit keen, and perceiving that the strength of the prisoner began to fail, instantly sunk their tomahawks in her head and left her, still warm and bleeding, upon the snow.

"As the whites came up, she retained strength enough to wave her hand in token of recognition, and appeared desirous of giving them some information with regard to the enemy, but her strength was too far gone. Her brother sprung from his horse and knelt by her side, endeavoring to stop the effusion of blood, but in vain. She gave him her hand, muttered some inarticulate words, and expired within two minutes after the arrival of the party. The pursuit was renewed with additional ardor, and in twenty minutes the enemy was within view. They had taken possession of a steep narrow ridge, and seemed desirous of magnifying their numbers in the eyes of the whites, as they ran rapidly from tree to tree, and maintained a steady yell in their most appalling tones. The pursuers, however, were too experienced to be deceived by so common an artifice, and being satisfied that the number of the enemy must be inferior to their own, they dismounted, tied their horses, and flanking out in such a manner as to enclose the enemy, ascended the ridge as rapidly as was consistent with a due regard to the shelter of their persons.

"The firing quickly commenced, and now for the first time they discovered that only two Indians were opposed to them. They had voluntarily sacrificed themselves for the safety of the main body, and succeeded in delaying pursuit until their friends could reach the mountains. One of them was instantly shot dead, and the other was badly wounded, as was evident from the blood upon his blanket, as well as that which filled his tracks in the snow for a considerable distance. The pursuit was recommenced, and urged keenly until night, when the trail entered a running stream and was lost. On the following morning the snow had melted, and every trace of the enemy was obliterated. This affair must be regarded as highly honorable to the skill, address, and activity of the Indians; and the self-devotion of the rear-guard is a lively instance of that magnanimity of which they are at times capable, and which is more remarkable in them, from the extreme caution and tende- regard for their own lives which usually distin- guished their warriors."

From this time Simon Kenton's name became very prominent as a leader. This year, at the head of forty-six men, he pursued a body of Indians, but did not succeed in overtaking them, which he afterward regarded as a fortunate cir- cumstance, as he ascertained that they were at least double the number of his own party. A man by the name of Scott, having been carried off by the Indians, Kenton followed them over the Ohio, and released him.

As early as January, 1788, the Indians entered Kentucky, two of them were captured near Crab Orchard by Captain Whitley. The same month, a party stole a number of horses from the Elkhorn settlements, they were pursued and surprised in their camp. Their leader extricated his band, by a singular stratagem. Springing up before the whites could fire, he went through a series of the most extraordinary antics, leaping and yelling as if frantic. This conduct absorbing the attention of the whites, his followers took advantage of the opportunity to escape As soon as they had all disappeared, the wily chief plunged into the woods and was seen no more. The attacks were continued in March. Several parties and families suffered severely. Lieutenant McClure, following the trail of a marauding party of Indians, fell in with another body, and, in the skirmish that ensued, was mortally wounded.

In 1789, a conference was held at the mouth of the Muskingum, with most of the north-western tribes, the result of which was the conclusion of another treaty. The Shawanese were not included in this pacification. This tribe was the most constant in its enmity to the whites, of all the Western Indians. There was but little use in making peace with the Indians unless all were included; for as long as one tribe was at war, restless spirits among the others were found to take part with them, and the whites, on the other hand, were not particular to distinguish between hostile and friendly Indians.

Though the depredations continued this year,

no affair of unusual interest occurred; small parties of the Indians infested the settlements, murdering and plundering the inhabitants. They were generally pursued, but mostly without success. Major McMillan was attacked by six or seven Indians, but escaped unhurt after killing two of his assailants.

A boat upon the Ohio was fired upon, five men killed, and a woman made prisoner. In their attacks upon boats, the Indians employed the stratagem of which the whites had been warned by Girty. White men would appear upon the shore, begging the crew to rescue them from the Indians, who were pursuing them. Some of these were renegades, and others prisoners compelled to act this part, under threats of death in its most dreadful form if they refused.

The warning of Girty is supposed to have saved many persons from this artifice; but too often unable to resist the many appeals, emigrants became victims to the finest feelings of our nature.

Thus in March, 1790, a boat descending the

river was decoyed ashore, and no sooner had it reached the bank than it was captured by fifty Indians, who killed a man and a woman, and made the rest prisoners. An expedition was made against the Indians on the Sciota by General Harmer, of the United States army, and General Scott, of the Kentucky militia, but nothing of consequence was achieved. In May a number of people returning from Divine service, on Bear Grass Creek, were attacked, and one man killed, and a woman made prisoner, who was afterward tomahawked. Three days after, a boat containing six men and several families was captured by sixteen Indians without loss. The whites were all carried off by the Indians, who intended, it is said, to make them slaves; one of the men escaped and brought the news to the settlements.

In the fall Harmer made a second expedition which was attended with great disasters. Several marauding attacks of the Indians ensued; nor was peace finally restored until after the treaty of Greenville, which followed the subjugation of the Indians by General Wayne in 1794.

CHAPTER XXI.

Colonel Boone meets with the loss of all his land in Kentucky, and emigrates to Virginia—Resides on the Kanawha, near Point Pleasant—Hears of the fertility of Missouri, and the abundance of game there—Emigrates to Missouri—Is appointed commandant of a district under the Spanish Government—Mr. Audubon's narrative of a night passed with Boone, and the narratives made by him during the night Extraordinary power of his memory.

A PERIOD of severe adversity for Colonel Boone now ensued. His aversion to legal tech nicalities and his ignorance of legal forms were partly the cause of defects in the titles to the lands which he had long ago acquired, improved, and nobly defended. But the whole system of land titles in Kentucky at that early period was so utterly defective, that hundreds of others who were better informed and more careful than the old pioneer, lost their lands by litigation and the arts and rogueries of land speculators, who made it their business to hunt up defects in land titles.

327

The Colonel lost all his land—even his beautiful farm near Boonesborough, which ought to have been held sacred by any men possessed of a particle of patriotism or honest feeling, was taken from him. He consequently left Kentucky and settled on the Kanawha River in Virginia, not far from Point Pleasant. This removal appears to have taken place in the year 1790. He remained in this place several years, cultivating a farm, raising stock, and at the proper seasons indulging in his favorite sport of hunting.

Some hunters who had been pursuing their sport on the western shores of the Missouri River gave Colonel Boone a very vivid description of that country, expatiating on the fertility of the land, the abundance of game, and the great herds of buffalo ranging over the vast expanse of the prairies. They also described the simple manners of the people, the absence of lawyers and lawsuits, and the Arcadian happiness which was enjoyed by all in the distant region, in such glowing terms that Boone resolved to emigrate and settle there, leaving his fourth son Jesse in the Kanawha valley, where he had married and settled, and who did not follow him till several years after.*

Mr. Peck fixes the period of this emigration in 1795, Perkins, in his " Western Annals," places it in 1797. His authority is an article of Thomas J. Hinde in the " American Pioneer," who says : " I was neighbor to Daniel Boone, the first white man that fortified against the Indians in Kentucky. In October, 1797, I saw him on pack-horses take up his journey for Missouri, then Upper Louisiana."

Mr. Peck says : † " At that period, and for several years after, the country of his retreat belonged to the Crown of Spain. His fame had reached this remote region before him; and he received of the Lieutenant-Governor, who resided at St. Louis, " assurance that ample portions of land should be given to him and his family." His first residence was in the Femme Osage settlement, in the District of St. Charles, about forty-five miles west of St. Louis. Here he remained with his son Daniel M. Boone until

* Peck. † Life of Boone.

1804, when he removed to the residence of his youngest son, Nathan Boone, with whom he continued till about 1810, when he went to reside with his son-in-law, Flanders Callaway. A commission from Don Charles D. Delassus, Lieutenant-Governor, dated July 11th, 1800, appointing him commandant of the Femme Osage District, was tendered and accepted. He retained this command, which included both civil and military duties, and he continued to discharge them with credit to himself, and to the satisfaction of all concerned, until the transfer of the government to the United States. The simple manners of the frontier people of Missouri exactly suited the peculiar habits and temper of Colonel Boone."

It was during his residence in Missouri that Colonel Boone was visited by the great naturalist, J. J. Audubon, who passed a night with him. In his Ornithological Biography, Mr. Audubon gives the following narrative of what passed on that occasion :

"Daniel Boone, or, as he was usually called in the Western country, Colonel Boone, happened to spend a night with me under the same roof, more than twenty years ago.* We had returned from a shooting excursion, in the course of which his extraordinary skill in the management of the rifle had been fully displayed. On retiring to the room appropriated to that remarkable individual and myself for the night, I felt anxious to know more of his exploits and adventures than I did, and accordingly took the liberty of proposing numerous questions to him. The stature and general appearance of this wanderer of the Western forests approached the gigantic. His chest was broad and prominent ; his muscular powers displayed themselves in every limb ; his countenance gave indication of his great courage, enterprise, and perseverance ; and when he spoke, the very motion of his lips brought the impression that whatever he uttered could not be otherwise than strictly true. 1 undressed, whilst he merely took off his hunting-shirt, and arranged a few folds of blankets on the floor, choosing rather to lie there, as he observed, than on the softest bed. When we

* This would be about the year 1810

had both disposed of ourselves, each after his own fashion, he related to me the following account of his powers of memory, which I lay before you, kind reader, in his own words, hoping that the simplicity of his style may prove interesting to you.

"'I was once,' said he, 'on a hunting expedition on the banks of the Green River, when the lower parts of this State (Kentucky) were still in the hands of nature, and none but the sons of the soil were looked upon as its lawful proprietors. We Virginians had for some time been waging a war of intrusion upon them, and I, amongst the rest, rambled through the woods in pursuit of their race, as I now would follow the tracks of any ravenous animal. The Indians outwitted me one dark night, and I was as unexpectedly as suddenly made a prisoner by them. The trick had been managed with great skill; for no sooner had I extinguished the fire of my camp, and laid me down to rest, in full security, as I thought, than I felt myself seized by an indistinguishable number of hands, and was immediately pinioned, as if about to be led to the scaffold for execution. To have attempted to be refractory would have proved useless and dangerous to my life ; and I suffered myself to be removed from my camp to theirs, a few miles distant, without uttering even a word of complaint. You are aware, I dare say, that to act in this manner was the best policy, as you understand that by so doing I proved to the Indians at once that I was born and bred as fearless of death as any of themselves.

"'When we reached the camp, great rejoicings were exhibited. Two squaws and a few papooses appeared particularly delighted at the sight of me, and I was assured, by very unequivocal gestures and words, that, on the morrow, the mortal enemy of the Red-skins would cease to live. I never opened my lips but was busy contriving some scheme which might enable me to give the rascals the slip before dawn. The women immediately fell a-searching about my hunting-shirt for whatever they might think valuable and, fortunately for me, soon found my flask filled with *Monongahela* (that is, reader, strong whisky). A terrific grin was exhibited on their murderous countenances, while my heart throbbed with joy at the anticipation of their intoxication. The crew immediately began to beat their bellies and sing, as they passed the bottle from mouth to mouth. How often did I wish the flask ten times its size, and filled with aquafortis! I observed that the squaws drank more freely than the warriors, and again my spirits were about to be depressed, when the report of a gun was heard at a distance. The Indians all jumped on their feet. The singing and drinking were both brought to a stand, and I saw, with inexpressible joy, the men walk off to some distance and talk to the squaws. I knew that they were consulting about me, and I foresaw that in a few moments the warriors would go to discover the cause of the gun having been fired so near their camp. I expected that the squaws would be left to guard me. Well, sir, it was just so. They returned; the men took up their guns, and walked away. The squaws sat down again, and in less than five minutes had my bottle up to their dirty mouths, gurgling down their throats the remains of the whisky.

" ' With what pleasure did I see them becoming more and more drunk, until the liquor took such hold of them that it was quite impossible for these women to be of any service. They tumbled down, rolled about, and began to snore; when I, having no other chance of freeing myself from the cords that fastened me, rolled over and over toward the fire, and, after a short time, burned them asunder. I rose on my feet, stretched my stiffened sinews, snatched up my rifle, and for once in my life spared that of Indians. I now recollect how desirous I once or twice felt to lay open the skulls of the wretches with my tomahawk; but when I again thought upon killing beings unprepared and unable to defend themselves, it looked like murder without need, and I gave up the idea.

" ' But, sir, I felt determined to mark the spot, and walking to a thrifty ash sapling I cut out of it three large chips, and ran off. I soon reached the river, soon crossed it, and threw myself deep into the canebrakes, imitating the tracks of an Indian with my feet so that no chance might be left for those from whom I had escaped to overtake me.

" ' It is now nearly twenty years since this happened, and more than five since I left the whites' settlements, which I might probably never have visited again had I not been called on as a witness in a lawsuit that was pending in Kentucky, and which I really believe would never have been settled had I not come forward and established the beginning of a certain boundary line.   This is the story, sir :

" ' Mr. —— moved from Old Virginia into Kentucky, and having a large tract granted to him in the new State, laid claim to a certain parcel of land adjoining Green River, and, as chance would have it, took for one of his corners the very ash tree on which I had made my mark, and finished his survey of some thousands of acres, beginning, as it is expressed in the deed, " at an ash marked by three distinct notches of the tomahawk of a white man."

" ' The tree had grown much, and the bark had covered the marks ; but, somehow or other, Mr.

—— heard from some one all that I have already said to you, and thinking that I might remember the spot alluded to in the deed, but which was no longer discoverable, wrote for me to come and try at least to find the place or the tree. His letter mentioned that all my expenses should be paid, and not caring much about once more going back to Kentucky I started and met Mr. ——. After some conversation, the affair with the Indians came to my recollection. I considered for a while, and began to think that after all I could find the very spot, as well as the tree, if it was yet standing.

" 'Mr. —— and I mounted our horses, and off we went to the Green River Bottoms. After some difficulties—for you must be aware, sir, that great changes have taken place in those woods—I found at last the spot where I had crossed the river, and, waiting for the moon to rise, made for the course in which I thought the ash tree grew. On approaching the place, I felt as if the Indians were there still, and as if I was still a prisoner among them. Mr. —— and

I camped near what I conceived the spot, and waited until the return of day.

"'At the rising of the sun I was on foot, and, after a good deal of musing, thought that an ash tree then in sight must be the very one on which I had made my mark. I felt as if there could be no doubt of it, and mentioned my thought to Mr. ——. " Well, Colonel Boone," said he, " if you think so, I hope it may prove true, but we must have some witnesses; do you stay here about and I will go and bring some of the settlers whom I know." I agreed. Mr. —— trotted off, and I, to pass the time, rambled about to see if a deer was still living in the land. But ah! sir, what a wonderful difference thirty years make in the country! Why, at the time when I was caught by the Indians, you would not have walked out in any direction for more than a mile without shooting a buck or a bear. There were then thousands of buffaloes on the hills in Kentucky; the land looked as if it never would become poor; and to hunt in those days was a pleasure indeed. But when I was left to myself on the banks of Green River, I dare say for the last time in my life, a few *signs* only of deer were to be seen, and, as to a deer itself, I saw none.

" ' Mr. —— returned, accompanied by three gentlemen. They looked upon me as if I had been Washington himself, and walked to the ash tree, which I now called my own, as if in quest of a long-lost treasure. I took an ax from one of them, and cut a few chips off the bark. Still no signs were to be seen. So I cut again until I thought it was time to be cautious, and I scraped and worked away with my butcher-knife until I *did* come to where my tomahawk had left an impression in the wood. We now went regularly to work, and scraped at the tree with care until three hacks, as plain as any three notches ever were, could be seen. Mr. —— and the other gentlemen were astonished, and I must allow I was as much surprised as pleased myself. I made affidavit of this remarkable occurrence in presence of these gentlemen. Mr.—— gained his cause. I left Green River forever, and came to where we now are and, sir, I wish you a good-night.' "

CHAPTER XXII.

Colonel Boone receives a large grant of land from the Spanish Government of Upper Louisiana—He subsequently loses it by neglecting to secure the formal title—His lawsuits in his new home—Character of the people—Sketch of the history of Missouri—Colonel Boone's hunting—He pays his debts by the sale of furs—Hunting excursions continued—In danger from the Indians—Taken sick in his hunting camp—His relatives settled in his neighborhood—Colonel Boone applies to Congress to recover his land—The Legislature of Kentucky supports his claim—Death of Mrs. Boone—Results of the application to Congress—He receives one-eleventh part of his just claim—He ceases to hunt—Occupations of his declining years—Mr. Harding paints his portrait.

In consideration of his official services as Syndic, ten thousand arpents* of excellent land were given to Colonel Boone by the Government. Under the special law, in order to make his title good, he should have obtained a confirmation of his grant from the immediate representative of the Crown, then residing in New

* An arpent of land is eighty-five hundredths of an acre.
340

Orleans. But his friend, the Commandant at St. Louis, undertook to dispense with his residence on the land which was another condition to a sound title, and Boone probably supposed that "all would be right" without attending to any of the formalities, and neglected to take the necessary steps for holding his land securely.

It is probable that he foresaw that Missouri would soon become a part of the United States, and expected justice from that quarter. But in this he was disappointed, for when that event took place, the commissioners of the United States appointed to decide on confirmed claims felt constrained by their instructions and rejected Colonel Boone's claims for want of legal formalities.

Thus was the noble pioneer a second time deprived of the recompense of his inestimable services by his inattention to the precaution necessary for securing his rights. This second misfortune came upon him some time after the period of which we are now writing.

Meantime Colonel Boone found his residence in Missouri agreeable, and in every respect congenial to his habits and tastes. His duties as Syndic were light; and he was allowed ample time for the cultivation of his land, and for occasional tours of hunting, in which he so greatly delighted. Trapping beaver was another of his favorite pursuits, and in this new country he found abundance of this as well as other species of game.

A greater part of the people of Missouri were emigrants from the United States, pioneers of the West, who had already resisted Indian aggressions, and were welcome by the French and Spanish settlers as a clear accession to their military strength.

A brief notice of the history of this State, showing how the different kinds of population came there, will be not inappropriate in this place.

Though the French were the first settlers, and for a long time the principal inhabitants of Missouri, yet a very small portion of her present population is of that descent. A fort was built by that people as early as 1719, near the site of the present capital, called Fort Orleans, and its lead mines worked to some extent the next year. St. Genevieve, the oldest town in the State, was settled in 1755, and St. Louis in 1764. At the treaty of 1763 it was assigned, with all the territory west of the Mississippi, to Spain. "In 1780, St. Louis was besieged and attacked by a body of British troops and Indians, fifteen hundred and forty strong." During the siege, sixty of the French were killed. The siege was raised by Colonel George Rogers Clark, who came with five hundred men to the relief of the place. At the close of the American Revolution, the territory west of the Mississippi remained with Spain till it was ceded to France, in 1801. In 1803, at the purchase of Louisiana, it came into the possession of the United States, and formed part of the territory of Louisiana until the formation of the State of that name in 1812, when the remainder of the territory was named Missouri, from which (after a stormy debate in Congress as to the admission of slavery) was separated the present State of Missouri in 1721.*

* Lippincott's Gazetteer.

The office of Syndic, to which Colonel Boone had been appointed, is similar to that of justice of the peace under our own government: but it is more extensive, as combining military with civil powers. Its exercise in Colonel Boone's district did not by any means occupy the whole of his time and attention. On the contrary, he found sufficient time for hunting in the winter months—the regular hunting season. At first he was not very successful in obtaining valuable furs, but after two or three seasons he was able to secure a sufficient quantity to enable him, by the proceeds of their sale, to discharge some outstanding debts in Kentucky; and he made a journey thither for that purpose. When he had seen each creditor, and paid him all he demanded, he returned home to Missouri, and on his arrival he had but half a dollar remaining. "To his family," says Mr. Peck, " and a circle of friends who had called to see him, he said, 'Now I am ready and willing to die. I am relieved from a burden that has long oppressed me. I have paid all my debts, and no one will say, when I am gone. "Boone was a dishonest man." I am perfectly willing to die." *

Boone still continued his hunting excursions, attended sometimes by some friend: but most frequently by a black servant boy. On one of these occasions these two had to resist an attack of Osage Indians, whom they speedily put to flight. At another time, when he was entirely alone, a large encampment of Indians made its appearance in his neighborhood; and he was compelled to secrete himself for twenty days in his camp cooking his food only in the middle of the night, so that the smoke of his fire would not be seen. At the end of this long period of inaction the Indians went off.

At another time, while in his hunting camp, with only a negro boy for his attendant, he fell sick and lay a long time unable to go out. When sufficiently recovered to walk out, he pointed out to the boy a place where he wished to be buried if he should die in camp, and also gave

* The owners of the money of which he was robbed on his journey to Virginia, as already related, had voluntarily relinquished all claims on him. This was a simple act of justice.

the boy very exact directions about his burial, and the disposal of his rifle, blankets and peltry.*

Among the relations of Colonel Boone, who were settled in his neighborhood, were Daniel Morgan Boone, his eldest son then living, who had gone out before his father; Nattra, with his wife, who had followed in 1800; and Flanders Callaway, his son-in-law, who had come out about the time that Missouri, then Upper Louisiana, became a part of the United States territory.†

We have already stated that the land granted to Colonel Boone, in consideration of his performing the duties of Syndic, was lost by his omission to comply with the legal formalities necessary to secure his title.

In addition to the ten thousand arpents of land thus lost, he had been entitled as a citizen to one thousand arpents of land according to the usage in other cases; but he appears not to have complied with the condition of actual residence on this land, and it was lost in consequence.

* Peck. † Ibid.

In 1812, Colonel Boone sent a petition to Congress praying for a confirmation of his orig. inal claims. In order to give greater weight to his application, he presented a memorial to the General Assembly of Kentucky, on the thir teenth of January, 1812, soliciting the aid of that body in obtaining from Congress the con firmation of his claims.

The Legislature, by a unanimous vote, passed the following preamble and resolutions :

"The Legislature of Kentucky, taking into view the many eminent services rendered by Col. Boone, in exploring and settling the western country, from which great advantages have re sulted, not only to this State, but to his country in general; and that from circumstances over which he had no control, he is now reduced to poverty, not having, so far as appears, an acre of land out of the vast territory he has been a great instrument in peopling; believing, also, that it is as unjust as it is impolitic, that useful enterprise and eminent services should go unre warded by a government where merit confers the only distinction; and having sufficient reason to believe that a grant of ten thousand acres of land, which he claims in Upper Louisiana, would have been confirmed by the Spanish government, had not said territory passed, by cession, into the hands of the general government: wherefore,

"Resolved, by the General Assembly of the Commonwealth of Kentucky,—That our Senators in Congress be requested to make use of their exertions to procure a grant of land in said territory to said Boone, either the ten thousand acres to which he appears to have an equitable claim, from the grounds set forth to this Legislature, by way of confirmation, or to such quantity in such place as shall be deemed most advisable, by way of donation."

Notwithstanding this action of the Legislature of Kentucky, Colonel Boone's appeal, like many other just and reasonable claims presented to Congress, was neglected for some time. During this period of anxious suspense, Mrs. Boone, the faithful and affectionate wife of the venerable pioneer, who had shared his toils and anxieties, and cheered his home for so many years, was taken from his side. She died in March, 1813, at the age of seventy-six. The venerable pioneer was now to miss her cheerful companionship for the remainder of his life; and to a man of his affectionate disposition this must have been a severe privation.

Colonel Boone's memorial to Congress received the earnest and active support of Judge Coburn, Joseph Vance, Judge Burnett, and other distinguished men belonging to the Western country. But it was not till the 24th of December, 1813, that the Committee on Public Lands made a report on the subject.

The report certainly is a very inconsistent one, as it fully admits the justice of his claim to eleven thousand arpents of land, and recommends Congress to give him the miserable pittance of one thousand arpents, to which he was entitled in common with all the other emigrants to Upper Louisiana! The act for the confirmation of the title passed on the 10th of February, 1814.

For ten years before his decease, Colonel Boone gave up his favorite pursuit of hunting.

The infirmities of age rendered it imprudent for him to venture alone in the woods.

The closing years of Colonel Boone's life were passed in a manner entirely characteristic of the man. He appears to have considered love to mankind, reverence to the Supreme Being, delight in his works and constant usefulness, as the legitimate ends of life. After the decease of Mrs. Boone, he divided his time among the different members of his family, making his home with his eldest daughter, Mrs. Callaway, visiting his other children, and especially his youngest son, Major Nathan Boone, for longer or shorter periods, according to his inclination and convenience. He was greatly beloved by all his descendants, some of whom were of the fifth generation; and he took great delight in their society.

"His time at home," says Mr. Peck, "was usually occupied in some useful manner. He made powder-horns for his grandchildren, neighbors, and friends, many of which were carved and ornamented with much taste. He repaired rifles, and performed various descriptions of handicraft with neatness and finish. Making powder-horns—repairing rifles—employments in pleasing unison with old pursuits. and by the associations thus raised in his mind, always recalling the pleasures of the chase, the stilly whispering hum of the pines, the fragrance of wild flowers, and the deep solitude of the primeval forest."

In the summer of 1820, Chester Harding, who of American artists is one of the most celebrated for the accuracy of his likenesses, paid a visit to Colonel Boone for the purpose of taking his portrait. The Colonel was quite feeble, and had to be supported by a friend, the Rev. J. E. Welsh, while sitting to the artist.*

This portrait is the original from which most of the engravings of Boone have been executed. It represents him in his hunting dress, with his large hunting-knife in his belt. The face is very thin and pale, and the hair perfectly white, the eyes of a bright blue color, and the expression of the countenance mild and pleasing.

* Peck. Life of Boone.

CHAPTER XXIII.

Last illness, and death of Colonel Boone—His funeral—Account of his family—His remains and those of his wife removed from Missouri, and reinterred in the new cemetery in Frankfort, Kentucky—Character of Colonel Boone.

In September, 1820, Colonel Boone had an attack of fever, from which he recovered so as to make a visit to the house of his son, Major Nathan Boone. Soon after, from an indiscretion in his diet, he had a relapse ; and after a confinement to the house of only three days, he expired on the 26th of September, in the eighty-sixth year of his age.

He was buried in a coffin which he had kept ready for several years. His remains were laid by the side of those of his deceased wife. The great respect and reverence entertained toward him, attracted a large concourse from the neighboring country to the funeral. The Legislature of Missouri, then in session, passed a resolution that the members should wear the badge of mourning usual in such cases for twenty days; and an adjournment for one day took place.

Colonel Boone had five sons and four daughters. The two oldest sons, as already related, were killed by the Indians. His third, Colonel Daniel Morgan Boone, resided in Missouri, and died about 1842, past the age of eighty. Jesse Boone, the fourth son, settled in Missouri about 1805, and died at St. Louis a few years after. Major Nathan Boone, the youngest child, resided for many years in Missouri, and received a commission in the United States Dragoons. He was still living at a recent date. Daniel Boone's daughters, Jemima, Susannah, Rebecca, and Lavinia, were all married, lived and died in Kentucky.

In 1845 the citizens of Frankfort, Kentucky, having prepared a rural cemetery, resolved to consecrate it by interring in it the remains of Daniel Boone and his wife. The consent of the family being obtained the reinterment took place on the 20th of August of that year.

The pageant was splendid and deeply interesting. A few survivors of Boone's contemporaries were present, gathered from all parts of the State, and a numerous train of his descendants and relatives led the van of the procession escorting the hearse, which was decorated with forest evergreens and white lilies, an appropriate tribute to the simple as well as glorious character of Boone, and suitable emblem of his enduring fame. The address was delivered by Mr. Crittenden, and the concourse of citizens from Kentucky and the neighboring States was immense.

The reader of the foregoing pages will have no difficulty in forming a correct estimate of Boone's character. He was one of the purest and noblest of the pioneers of the West. Regarding himself as an instrument in the hands of Providence for accomplishing great purposes, he was nevertheless always modest and unassuming, never seeking distinction, but always accepting the post of duty and danger.

As a military leader he was remarkable for prudence, coolness, bravery, and imperturbable self-possession. His knowledge of the character

of the Indians enabled him to divine their intentions and baffle their best laid plans ; and
notwithstanding his resistance of their inroads,
he was always a great favorite amongst them.
As a father, husband, and citizen his character
seems to have been faultless ; and his intercourse
with his fellow-men was always marked by the
strictest integrity and honor.

COLONEL BOONE'S AUTOBIOGRAPHY.

[The following pages were dictated by Colonel Boone to John
Filson, and published in 1784. Colonel Boone has been
heard to say repeatedly since its publication, that "it is
every word true."]

CURIOSITY is natural to the soul of man, and interesting objects have a powerful influence on our
affections. Let these influencing powers actuate, by
the permission or disposal of Providence, from self-
ish or social views, yet in time the mysterious will
of Heaven is unfolded, and we behold our conduct,
from whatsoever motives excited, operating to answer the important designs of Heaven. Thus we
behold Kentucky, lately a howling wilderness, the
habitation of savages and wild beasts, become a
fruitful field; this region, so favorably distinguished
by nature, now become the habitation of civilization,
at a period unparalleled in history, in the midst of
a raging war, and under all the disadvantages of
emigration to a country so remote from the inhabited parts of the continent. Here, where the hand
of violence shed the blood of the innocent; where
the horrid yells of savages and the groans of the

357

distressed sounded in our ears, we now hear the praises and adorations of our Creator; where wretched wigwams stood, the miserable abodes of savages, we behold the foundations of cities laid, that, in all probability, will equal the glory of the greatest upon earth. And we view Kentucky, situated on the fertile banks of the great Ohio, rising from obscurity to shine with splendor, equal to any other of the stars of the American hemisphere.

The settling of this region well deserves a place in history. Most of the memorable events I have myself been exercised in and, for the satisfaction of the public, will briefly relate the circumstance of my adventures, and scenes of life from my first movement to this country until this day.

It was on the first of May, in the year 1769, that I resigned my domestic happiness for a time, and left my family and peaceable habitation on the Yadkin River, in North Carolina, to wander through the wilderness of America, in quest of the country of Kentucky, in company with John Finley, John Stewart, Joseph Holden, James Monay, and William Cool. We proceeded successfully, and after a long and fatiguing journey through a mountainous wilderness, in a westward direction. On the 7th of June following we found ourselves on Red River, where John Finley had formerly been trading with the Indians, and, from the top of an eminence, saw with pleasure the beautiful level of Kentucky. Here let me observe that for some time we had experienced the most uncomfortable weather, as a prelibation of our future sufferings.   At this place we encamped, and made a shelter to defend us from the inclement season, and began to hunt and reconnoiter the country.   We found everywhere abundance of wild beasts of all sorts, through this vast forest.   The buffalo were more frequent than I have seen cattle in the settlements, browsing on the leaves of the cane, or cropping the herbage on those extensive plains, fearless, because ignorant of the violence of man.   Sometimes we saw hundreds in a drove, and the numbers about the salt springs were amazing.   In this forest, the habitation of beasts of every kind natural to America, we practised hunting with great success until the 22d day of December following.

This day John Stewart and I had a pleasing ramble, but fortune changed the scene in the close of it. We had passed through a great forest, on which stood myriads of trees, some gay with blossoms, and others rich with fruits.   Nature was here a series of wonders, and a fund of delight.   Here she displayed her ingenuity and industry in a variety of flowers and fruits, beautifully colored, elegantly shaped, and charmingly flavored; and we were diverted with innumerable animals presenting themselves perpetually to our view.   In the decline of the day, near Kentucky River, as we ascended the brow of a small hill, a number of Indians rushed out of a thick cane-brake upon us, and made us prisoners.   The time of our sorrow was now arrived, and the scene fully opened.   The Indians plundered us of what we had, and kept us in confinement seven days, treating us with common savage usage. During this time we discovered no uneasiness or desire to escape, which made them less suspicious of us; but in the dead of night, as we lay in a thick canebrake by a large fire, when sleep had locked up their senses, my situation not disposing me for rest, I touched my companion and gently awoke him. We improved this favorable opportunity and departed, leaving them to take their rest, and speedily directed our course toward our old camp, but found it plundered, and the company dispersed and gone home. About this time my brother, Squire Boone, with another adventurer, who came to explore the country shortly after us, was wandering through the forest, determined to find me if possible, and accidentally found our camp. Notwithstanding the unfortunate circumstances of our company, and our dangerous situation, as surrounded with hostile savages, our meeting so fortunately in the wilderness made us reciprocally sensible of the utmost satisfaction. So much does friendship triumph over misfortune, that sorrows and sufferings vanish at the meeting not only of real friends, but of the most distant acquaintances, and substitute happiness in their room.

Soon after this, my companion in captivity, John Stewart, was killed by the savages, and the man that came with my brother returned home by himself. We were then in a dangerous, helpless situation, exposed daily to perils and death among savages and wild beasts—not a white man in the country but ourselves.

Thus situated, many hundred miles from our families in the howling wilderness, I believe few would have equally enjoyed the happiness we experienced. I often observed to my brother, " You see now how little nature requires to be satisfied. Felicity, the companion of content, is rather found in our own breasts than in the enjoyment of external things; and I firmly believe it requires but a little philosophy to make a man happy in whatsoever state he is. This consists in a full resignation to the will of Providence; and a resigned soul finds pleasure in a path strewed with briers and thorns."

We continued in a state of indolence, but hunted every day, and prepared a little cottage to defend us from the winter storms. We remained there undisturbed during the winter, and on the first day of May, 1770, my brother returned home to the settlement by himself, for a new recruit of horses and ammunition, leaving me by myself, without bread, salt, or sugar, without company of my fellow-creatures, or even a horse or dog. I confess I never before was under greater necessity of exercising philosophy and fortitude. A few days I passed uncomfortably. The idea of a beloved wife and family, and their anxiety upon the account of my absence and exposed situation, made sensible impressions on my heart. A thousand dreadful apprehensions presented themselves to my view, and had undoubtedly disposed me to melancholy, if further indulged.

One day I undertook a tour through the country,

and the diversity and beauties of nature I met with in this charming season expelled every gloomy and vexatious thought. Just at the close of day the gentle gales retired, and left the place to the disposal of a profound calm. Not a breeze shook the most tremulous leaf. I had gained the summit of a commanding ridge, and, looking round with astonishing delight, beheld the ample plains, the beauteous tracts below. On the other hand, I surveyed the famous river Ohio, that rolled in silent dignity, marking the western boundary of Kentucky with inconceivable grandeur. At a vast distance I beheld the mountains lift their venerable brows, and penetrate the clouds. All things were still. I kindled a fire near a fountain of sweet water, and feasted on the loin of a buck, which a few hours before I had killed. The sullen shades of night soon overspread the whole hemisphere, and the earth seemed to gasp after the hovering moisture. My roving excursion this day had fatigued my body, and diverted my imagination. I laid me down to sleep, and I awoke not until the sun had chased away the night. I continued this tour, and in a few days explored a considerable part of the country, each day equally pleased as the first. I returned again to my old camp, which was not disturbed in my absence. I did not confine my lodging to it, but often reposed in thick canebrakes, to avoid the savages, who, I believe, often visited my camp, but, fortunately for me, in my absence. In this situation I was constantly exposed to danger and death. How unhappy such a situation for a man tormented with fear, which is vain if no danger comes, and if it does, only augments the pain! It was my happiness to be destitute of this afflicting passion, with which I had the greatest reason to be affected. The prowling wolves diverted my nocturnal hours with perpetual howlings; and the various species of animals in this vast forest, in the daytime, were continually in my view.

Thus I was surrounded by plenty in the midst of want. I was happy in the midst of dangers and inconveniences. In such adversity, it was impossible I should be disposed to melancholy. No populous city, with all the varieties of commerce and stately structures, could afford so much pleasure to my mind as the beauties of nature I found here.

Thus, through an uninterrupted scene of sylvan pleasures, I spent the time until the 27th day of July following, when my brother, to my great felicity, met me, according to appointment, at our old camp. Shortly after, we left this place, not thinking it safe to stay there longer, and proceeded to Cumberland River, reconnoitering that part of the country until March, 1771, and giving names to the different waters.

Soon after, I returned home to my family, with a determination to bring them as soon as possible to live in Kentucky, which I esteemed a second paradise, at the risk of my life and fortune.

I returned safe to my old habitation, and found my family in happy circumstances. I sold my farm on the Yadkin, and what goods we could not carry with us; and on the 25th day of September, 1773, bade a farewell to our friends, and proceeded on our journey to Kentucky, in company with five families more, and forty men that joined us in Powell's Valley, which is one hundred and fifty miles from the now settled parts of Kentucky. This promising beginning was soon overcast with a cloud of adversity; for, upon the 10th day of October, the rear of our company was attacked by a number of Indians, who killed six and wounded one man. Of these, my eldest son was one that fell in the action. Though we defended ourselves and repulsed the enemy, yet this unhappy affair scattered our cattle, brought us into extreme difficulty, and so discouraged the whole company, that we retreated forty miles, to the settlement on Clinch River. We had passed over two mountains, viz., Powell's and Walden's, and were approaching Cumberland mountain when this adverse fortune overtook us. These mountains are in the wilderness, as we pass from the old settlements in Virginia to Kentucky, are ranged in a southwest and northwest direction, are of a great length and breadth, and not far distant from each other. Over these, nature hath formed passes that are less difficult than might be expected, from a view of such huge piles. The aspect of these cliffs is so wild and horrid, that it is impossible to behold them without terror. The spectator is apt to imagine that nature has formerly suffered some violent convulsion, and that these are the dismembered remains of the dreadful shock; the ruins, not of Persepolis or Palmyra, but of the world!

I remained with my family on Clinch until the 6th of June, 1774, when I and one Michael Stoner were solicited by Governor Dunmore of Virginia to go to the falls of the Ohio to conduct into the settlements a number of surveyors that had been sent thither by him some months before; this country having about this time drawn the attention of many adventurers. We immediately complied with the Governor's request, and conducted in the surveyors—completing a tour of eight hundred miles, through many difficulties, in sixty-two days.

Soon after I returned home, I was ordered to take the command of three garrisons during the campaign which Governor Dunmore carried on against the Shawanese Indians; after the conclusion of which, the militia was discharged from each garrison, and I, being relieved from my post, was solicited by a number of North Carolina gentlemen, that were about purchasing the lands lying on the south side of Kentucky River, from the Cherokee Indians, to attend their treaty at Wataga, in March, 1775, to negotiate with them, and mention the boundaries of the purchase. This I accepted; and, at the request of the same gentlemen, undertook to mark out a road in the best passage from the settlement through the wilderness to Kentucky, with such assistance as I thought necessary to employ for such an important undertaking.

I soon began this work, having collected a number

of enterprising men, well armed. We proceeded with all possible expedition until we came within fifteen miles of where Boonesborough now stands, and where we were fired upon by a party of Indians that killed two, and wounded two of our number; yet, although surprised and taken at a disadvantage, we stood our ground. This was on the 20th of March, 1775. Three days after, we were fired upon again, and had two men killed, and three wounded. Afterward we proceeded on to Kentucky River without opposition; and on the first day of April began to erect the fort Boonesborough at a salt lick, about sixty yards from the river, on the south side.

On the fourth day, the Indians killed one of our men. We were busily employed in building this fort until the fourteenth day of June following, without any further opposition from the Indians; and having finished the works, I returned to my family on Clinch.

In a short time I proceeded to remove my family from Clinch to this garrison, where we arrived safe, without any other difficulties than such as are common to this passage; my wife and daughter being the first white women that ever stood on the banks of Kentucky River.

On the 24th day of December following, we had one man killed, and one wounded by the Indians, who seemed determined to persecute us for erecting this fortification.

On the fourteenth day of July, 1776, two of

Colonel Calloway's daughters, and one of mine, were taken prisoners near the fort. I immediately pursued the Indians with only eight men, and on the 16th overtook them, killed two of the party, and recovered the girls. The same day on which this attempt was made, the Indians divided themselves into different parties, and attacked several forts, which were shortly before this time erected, doing a great deal of mischief. This was extremely distressing to the new settlers. The innocent husbandman was shot down, while busy in cultivating the soil for his family's supply. Most of the cattle around the stations were destroyed. They continued their hostilities in this manner until the 15th of April, 1777, when they attacked Boonesborough with a party of above one hundred in number, killed one man, and wounded four. Their loss in this attack was not certainly known to us.

On the 4th day of July following, a party of about two hundred Indians attacked Boonesborough, killed one man and wounded two. They besieged us forty-eight hours during which time seven of them were killed, and, at last, finding themselves not likely to prevail, they raised the siege and departed.

The Indians had disposed their warriors in different parties at this time, and attacked the different garrisons, to prevent their assisting each other, and did much injury to the distressed inhabitants.

On the 19th day of this month, Colonel Logan's fort was besieged by a party of about two hundred

Indians. During this dreadful siege they did a great deal of mischief, distressed the garrison, in which were only fifteen men, killed two, and wounded one. The enemy's loss was uncertain, from the common practise which the Indians have of carrying off their dead in time of battle. Colonel Harrod's fort was then defended by only sixty-five men, and Boonesborough by twenty-two, there being no more forts or white men in the country, except at the Falls, a considerable distance from these; and all, taken collectively, were but a handful to the numerous warriors that were everywhere dispersed through the country, intent upon doing all the mischief that savage barbarity could invent. Thus we passed through a scene of sufferings that exceeds description.

On the 25th of this month, a reinforcement of forty-five men arrived from North Carolina, and about the 20th of August following, Colonel Bowman arrived with one hundred men from Virginia. Now we began to strengthen; and hence, for the space of six weeks, we had skirmishes with Indians, in one quarter or another, almost every day.

The savages now learned the superiority of the Long Knife, as they call the Virginians, by experience; being out-generaled in almost every battle. Our affairs began to wear a new aspect, and the enemy, not daring to venture on open war, practised secret mischief at times.

On the 1st day of January, 1778, I went with a party of thirty men to the Blue Licks, on Licking

River, to make salt for the different garrisons in the country.

On the 7th day of February, as I was hunting to procure meat for the company, I met with a party of one hundred and two Indians, and two Frenchmen, on their march against Boonesborough, that place being particularly the object of the enemy. They pursued, and took me; and brought me on the 8th day to the Licks, where twenty-seven of my party were, three of them having previously returned home with the salt. I, knowing it was impossible for them to escape, capitulated with the enemy, and, at a distance, in their view, gave notice to my men of their situation, with orders not to resist, but surrender themselves captives.

The generous usage the Indians had promised before in my capitulation, was afterward fully complied with, and we proceeded with them as prisoners to Old Chillicothe, the principal Indian town on little Miami, where we arrived, after an uncomfortable journey, in very severe weather, on the 18th day of February, and received as good treatment as prisoners could expect from savages. On the 10th day of March following, I and ten of my men were conducted by forty Indians to Detroit, where we arrived the 30th day, and were treated by Governor Hamilton, the British commander at that post, with great humanity.

During our travels, the Indians entertained me well, and their affection for me was so great, that they utterly refused to leave me there with the others, although the Governor offered them one hundred pounds sterling for me, on purpose to give me a parole to go home. Several English gentlemen there, being sensible of my adverse fortune, and touched with human sympathy, generously offered a friendly supply for my wants, which I refused, with many thanks for their kindness—adding, that I never expected it would be in my power to recompense such unmerited generosity.

The Indians left my men in captivity with the British at Detroit, and on the 10th day of April brought me toward Old Chillicothe, where we arrived on the 25th day of the same month. This was a long and fatiguing march, through an exceedingly fertile country, remarkable for fine springs and streams of water. At Chillicothe I spent my time as comfortably as I could expect; was adopted, according to their custom, into a family, where I became a son, and had a great share in the affection of my new parents, brothers, sisters, and friends. I was exceedingly familiar and friendly with them, always appearing as cheerful and satisfied as possible, and they put great confidence in me. I often went a hunting with them, and frequently gained their applause for my activity at our shooting-matches. I was careful not to exceed many of them in shooting; for no people are more envious than they in this sport. I could observe, in their countenances and gestures, the greatest expressions of joy when they exceeded me; and, when the reverse happened, of envy. The Shawanese king took great notice of me, and treated me with profound respect and entire friendship, often intrusting me to hunt at my liberty. I frequently returned with the spoils of the woods, and as often presented some of what I had taken to him, expressive of duty to my sovereign. My food and lodging were in common with them; not so good, indeed, as I could desire, but necessity makes everything acceptable.

I now began to meditate an escape, and carefully avoided their suspicions, continuing with them at Old Chillicothe until the 1st day of June following, and then was taken by them to the salt springs on Scioto, and kept there making salt ten days. During this time I hunted some for them, and found the land, for a great extent about this river, to exceed the soil of Kentucky, if possible, and remarkably well watered.

When I returned to Chillicothe, alarmed to see four hundred and fifty Indians, of their choicest warriors, painted and armed in a fearful manner, ready to march against Boonesborough, I determined to escape the first opportunity.

On the 16th, before sunrise, I departed in the most secret manner, and arrived at Boonesborough on the 20th, after a journey of one hundred and sixty miles, during which I had but one meal.

I found our fortress in a bad state of defense; but we proceeded immediately to repair our flanks, strengthen our gates and posterns, and form double bastions, which we completed in ten days. In this time we daily expected the arrival of the Indian army; and at length, one of my fellow-prisoners, escaping from them, arrived, informing us that the enemy had, on account of my departure, postponed their expedition three weeks. The Indians had spies out viewing our movements, and were greatly alarmed with our increase in number and fortifications. The grand council of the nations were held frequently, and with more deliberation than usual. They evidently saw the approaching hour when the Long Knife would dispossess them of their desirable habitations; and, anxiously concerned for futurity, determined utterly to extirpate the whites out of Kentucky. We were not intimidated by their movements, but frequently gave them proofs of our courage.

About the first of August, I made an incursion into the Indian country with a party of nineteen men, in order to surprise a small town up Scioto, called Paint Creek Town. We advanced within four miles thereof, when we met a party of thirty Indians on their march against Boonesborough, intending to join the other from Chillicothe. A smart fight ensued between us for some time; at length the savages gave way and fled. We had no loss on our side; the enemy had one killed, and two wounded. We took from them three horses, and all their baggage; and being informed by two of our number that went to their town, that the Indians had entirely evacuated it, we proceeded no further, and returned with all possible expedition to assist our garrison against the other party. We passed by them on the sixth day, and on the seventh we arrived safe at Boonesborough.

On the 8th, the Indian army arrived, being four hundred and forty-four in number, commanded by Captain Duquesne, eleven other Frenchmen, and some of their own chiefs, and marched up within view of our fort, with British and French colors flying; and having sent a summons to me, in his Britannic Majesty's name, to surrender the fort, I requested two days' consideration, which was granted.

It was now a critical period with us. We were a small number in the garrison—a powerful army before our walls, whose appearance proclaimed inevitable death, fearfully painted, and marking their footsteps with desolation. Death was preferable to captivity; and if taken by storm, we must inevitably be devoted to destruction. In this situation we concluded to maintain our garrison, if possible. We immediately proceeded to collect what we could of our horses and other cattle, and bring them through the posterns into the fort; and in the evening of the 9th, I returned answer that we were determined to defend our fort while a man was living. "Now," said I to their commander, who stood attentively hearing my sentiments, "we laugh at your formidable preparations; but thank you for giving us notice and time to provide for our defense. Your efforts will not prevail; for our gates shall forever deny you admittance." Whether this answer affected their courage or not I cannot tell; but contrary to our expectations they formed a scheme to deceive us,

declaring it was their orders, from Governor Hamilton, to take us captives, and not to destroy us; but
if nine of us would come out and treat with them,
they would immediately withdraw their forces from
our walls, and return home peaceably. This sounded
grateful in our ears; and we agreed to the proposal.

We held the treaty within sixty yards of the
garrison, on purpose to divert them from a breach
of honor, as we could not avoid suspicions of the
savages. In this situation the articles were formally
agreed to, and signed; and the Indians told us it
was customary with them on such occasions for two
Indians to shake hands with every white man in the
treaty as an evidence of entire friendship. We
agreed to this also, but we were soon convinced their
policy was to take us prisoners. They immediately
grappled us; but, although surrounded by hundreds
of savages, we extricated ourselves from them, and
escaped all safe into the garrison, except one that
was wounded, through a heavy fire from their army.
They immediately attacked us on every side, and a
constant heavy fire ensued between us, day and
night, for the space of nine days.

At this time the enemy began to undermine our
fort, which was situated sixty yards from Kentucky
River. They began at the water-mark, and proceeded in the bank some distance, which we understood by their making the water muddy with the
clay; and we immediately proceeded to disappoint
their design, by cutting a trench across their sub-
terranean passage. The enemy, discovering our

countermine by the clay we threw out of the fort, desisted from that stratagem; and experience now fully convincing them that neither their power nor policy could effect their purpose, on the 20th day of August they raised the siege and departed.

During this siege, which threatened death in every form, we had two men killed, and four wounded, besides a number of cattle. We killed of the enemy thirty-seven, and wounded a great number. After they were gone, we picked up one hundred and twenty-five pounds' weight of bullets, besides what stuck in the logs of our fort, which certainly is a great proof of their industry. Soon after this, I went into the settlement, and nothing worthy of a place in this account passed in my affairs for some time.

During my absence from Kentucky, Colonel Bowman carried on an expedition against the Shawanese, at Old Chillicothe, with one hundred and sixty men, in July, 1779. Here they arrived undiscovered, and a battle ensued, which lasted until ten o'clock A. M., when Colonel Bowman, finding he could not succeed at this time, retreated about thirty miles. The Indians, in the meantime, collecting all their forces, pursued and overtook him, when a smart fight continued near two hours, not to the advantage of Colonel Bowman's party.

Colonel Harrod proposed to mount a number of horse, and furiously to rush upon the savages, who at this time fought with remarkable fury. This desperate step had a happy effect, broke their line of battle, and the savages fled on all sides. In these two battles we had nine killed, and one wounded. The enemy's loss uncertain, only two scalps being taken.

On the 22d day of June, 1780, a large party of Indians and Canadians, about six hundred in number, commanded by Colonel Byrd, attacked Ruddle's and Martin's stations, at the forks of Licking River, with six pieces of artillery. They carried this expedition so secretly, that the unwary inhabitants did not discover them until they fired upon the forts; and, not being prepared to oppose them, were obliged to surrender themselves miserable captives to barbarous savages, who immediately after tomahawked one man and two women, and loaded all the others with heavy baggage, forcing them along toward their towns, able and unable to march. Such as were weak and faint by the way, they tomahawked. The tender women and helpless children fell victims to their cruelty. This, and the savage treatment they received afterward, is shocking to humanity and too barbarous to relate.

The hostile disposition of the savages and their allies caused General Clarke, the commandant at the Falls of the Ohio, immediately to begin an expedition with his own regiment, and the armed force of the country, against Pecaway, the principal town of the Shawanese, on a branch of Great Miami, which he finished with great success, took seventeen scalps and burnt the town to ashes, with the loss of seventeen men.

About this time I returned to Kentucky with my family ; and here, to avoid an inquiry into my conduct, the reader being before informed of my bringing my family to Kentucky, I am under the necessity of informing him that, during my captivity with the Indians, my wife, who despaired of ever seeing me again—expecting the Indians had put a period to my life, oppressed with the distresses of the country, and bereaved of me, her only happiness—had, before I returned, transported my family and goods on horses through the wilderness, amid a multitude of dangers, to her father's house in North Carolina.

Shortly after the troubles at Boonesborough, I went to them, and lived peaceably there until this time. The history of my going home, and returning with my family, forms a series of difficulties, an account of which would swell a volume ; and, being foreign to my purpose, I shall purposely omit them.

I settled my family in Boonesborough once more ; and shortly after, on the 6th day of October, 1780, I went in company with my brother to the Blue Licks : and, on our return home, we were fired upon by a party of Indians. They shot him and pursued me, by the scent of their dog, three miles ; but I killed the dog, and escaped. The winter soon came on, and was very severe, which confined the Indians to their wigwams.

The severities of this winter caused great difficulties in Kentucky. The enemy had destroyed most of the corn the summer before. This necessary article was scarce and dear, and the inhabitants lived chiefly on the flesh of buffalo. The circumstances of many were very lamentable; however, being a hardy race of people, and accustomed to difficulties and necessities they were wonderfully supported through all their sufferings, until the ensuing autumn, when we received abundance from the fertile soil.

Toward spring we were frequently harassed by Indians; and in May, 1782, a party assaulted Ashton's station, killed one man, and took a negro prisoner. Captain Ashton, with twenty-five men, pursued and overtook the savages, and a smart fight ensued, which lasted two hours; but they, being superior in number, obliged Captain Ashton's party to retreat, with the loss of eight killed, and four mortally wounded; their brave commander himself being numbered among the dead.

The Indians continued their hostilities; and, about the 10th of August following, two boys were taken from Major Hoy's station. This party was pursued by Captain Holder and seventeen men, who were also defeated, with the loss of four men killed, and one wounded. Our affairs became more and more alarming. Several stations which had lately been erected in the country were continually infested with savages, stealing their horses and killing the men at every opportunity. In a field, near Lexington, an Indian shot a man, and running to scalp him, was himself shot from the fort, and fell dead upon his enemy.

Every day we experienced recent mischiefs. The barbarous savage nations of Shawanese, Cherokees,

Wyandots, Tawas, Delawares, and several others near Detroit, united in a war against us, and assembled their choicest warriors at Old Chillicothe, to go on the expedition, in order to destroy us, and entirely depopulate the country. Their savage minds were inflamed to mischief by two abandoned men, Captains M'Kee and Girty. These led them to execute every diabolical scheme, and on the 15th day of August, commanded a party of Indians and Canadians, of about five hundred in number, against Bryant's station, five miles from Lexington. Without demanding a surrender, they furiously assaulted the garrison, which was happily prepared to oppose them; and, after they had expended much ammunition in vain, and killed the cattle round the fort, not being likely to make themselves masters of this place, they raised the siege, and departed in the morning of the third day after they came, with the loss of about thirty killed, and the number of wounded uncertain. Of the garrison, four were killed, and three wounded.

On the 18th day, Colonel Todd, Colonel Trigg, Major Harland, and myself, speedily collected one hundred and seventy-six men well armed, and pursued the savages. They had marched beyond the Blue Licks, to a remarkable bend of the main fork of Licking River, about forty-three miles from Lexington, where we overtook them on the 19th day. The savages observing us, gave way; and we, being ignorant of their numbers, passed the river. When the enemy saw our proceedings,

having greatly the advantage of us in situation, they
formed the line of the battle from one bend of
Licking to the other, about a mile from the Blue
Licks. An exceeding fierce battle immediately
began, for about fifteen minutes, when we being
overpowered by numbers were obliged to retreat,
with the loss of sixty-seven men, seven of whom
were taken prisoners. The brave and much-lamented
Colonels Todd and Trigg, Major Harland, and my
second son, were among the dead. We were informed that the Indians, numbering their dead,
found they had four killed more than we; and therefore four of the prisoners they had taken were, by
general consent, ordered to be killed in a most barbarous manner by the young warriors, in order to
train them up to cruelty; and then they proceeded
to their towns.

On our retreat we were met by Colonel Logan,
hastening to join us, with a number of well-armed
men. This powerful assistance we unfortunately
wanted in the battle; for, notwithstanding the
enemy's superiority of numbers, they acknowledged
that, if they had received one more fire from us,
they should undoubtedly have given way. So
valiantly did our small party fight, that to the
memory of those who unfortunately fell in the
battle, enough of honor cannot be paid. Had
Colonel Logan and his party been with us, it is
highly probable we should have given the savages a
total defeat.

I cannot reflect upon this dreadful scene, but

sorrow fills my heart. A zeal for the defense of their country led these heroes to the scene of action, though with a few men to attack a powerful army of experienced warriors. When we gave way, they pursued us with the utmost eagerness, and in every quarter spread destruction. The river was difficult to cross, and many were killed in the flight—some just entering the river, some in the water, others after crossing, in ascending the cliffs. Some escaped on horseback, a few on foot; and, being dispersed everywhere in a few hours, brought the melancholy news of this unfortunate battle to Lexington. Many widows were now made. The reader may guess what sorrow filled the hearts of the inhabitants, exceeding anything that I am able to describe. Being reinforced, we returned to bury the dead and found their bodies strewed everywhere, cut and mangled in a dreadful manner. This mournful scene exhibited a horror almost unparalleled: some torn and eaten by wild beasts; those in the river eaten by fishes; all in such a putrefied condition, that no one could be distinguished from another.

As soon as General Clarke, then at the Falls of the Ohio—who was ever our ready friend, and merits the love and gratitude of all his countrymen—understood the circumstances of this unfortunate action, he ordered an expedition, with all possible haste, to pursue the savages, which was so expeditiously effected that we overtook them within two miles of their towns; and probably might have obtained a great victory, had not two of their number

met us about two hundred poles before we came up.
These returned quick as lightning to their camp, with
the alarming news of a mighty army in view. The
savages fled in the utmost disorder, evacuated their
towns, and reluctantly left their territory to our
mercy. We immediately took possession of Old
Chillicothe without opposition, being deserted by its
inhabitants. We continued our pursuit through five
towns on the Miami River, Old Chillicothe, Pecaway,
New Chillicothe, Will's Towns, and Chillicothe—
burnt them all to ashes, entirely destroyed their corn,
and other fruits, and everywhere spread a scene of
desolation in the country. In this expedition we took
seven prisoners and five scalps, with the loss of only
four men, two of whom were accidentally killed by
our own army.

This campaign in some measure damped the spirits
of the Indians, and made them sensible of our superiority. Their connections were dissolved, their
armies scattered, and a future invasion put entirely
out of their power; yet they continued to practise
mischief secretly upon the inhabitants, in the exposed parts of the country.

In October following, a party made an incursion
into that district called the Crab Orchard; and one
of them, being advanced some distance before the
others, boldly entered the house of a poor defenseless family, in which was only a negro man, a woman,
and her children, terrified with the apprehensions of
immediate death. The savage, perceiving their defenseless condition, without offering violence to the

family, attempted to capture the negro, who happily proved an overmatch for him, threw him on the ground, and in the struggle, the mother of the children drew an ax from a corner of the cottage, and cut his head off, while her little daughter shut the door. The savages instantly appeared, and applied their tomahawks to the door. An old rusty gun-barrel, without a lock, lay in a corner, which the mother put through a small crevice, and the savages, perceiving it, fled. In the meantime, the alarm spread through the neighborhood; the armed men collected immediately, and pursued the savages into the wilderness. Thus Providence, by the means of this negro, saved the whole of the poor family from destruction. From that time until the happy return of peace between the United States and Great Britain, the Indians did us no mischief. Finding the great king beyond the water disappointed in his expectations, and conscious of the importance of the Long Knife, and their own wretchedness, some of the nations immediately desired peace; to which, at present [1784], they seem universally disposed, and are sending ambassadors to General Clarke, at the Falls of the Ohio, with the minutes of their councils.

To conclude, I can now say that I have verified the saying of an old Indian who signed Colonel Henderson's deed. Taking me by the hand, at the delivery thereof—"Brother," said he, "we have given you a fine land, but I believe you will have much trouble in settling it." My footsteps have often

been marked with blood, and therefore I can truly
subscribe to its original name. Two darling sons
and a brother have I lost by savage hands, which
have also taken from me forty valuable horses, and
abundance of cattle. Many dark and sleepless nights
have I been a companion for owls, separated from
the cheerful society of men, scorched by the summer's
sun, and pinched by the winter's cold—an instrument ordained to settle the wilderness. But now
the scene is changed: peace crowns the sylvan
shade.

What thanks, what ardent and ceaseless thanks
are due to that all-superintending Providence which
has turned a cruel war into peace, brought order
out of confusion, made the fierce savages placid, and
turned away their hostile weapons from our country! May the same Almighty Goodness banish the
accursed monster, war, from all lands, with her
hated associates, rapine and insatiable ambition!
Let peace, descending from her native heaven, bid
her olives spring amid the joyful nations; and plenty,
in league with commerce, scatter blessings from her
copious hand!

This account of my adventures will inform the
reader of the most remarkable events of this country. I now live in peace and safety, enjoying the
sweets of liberty, and the bounties of Providence,
with my once fellow-sufferers, in this delightful
country, which I have seen purchased with a vast
expense of blood and treasure: delighting in the
prospect of its being, in a short time, one of the

most opulent and powerful States on the continent of North America; which, with the love and gratitude of my countrymen, I esteem a sufficient reward for all my toil and dangers.

DANIEL BOONE

Fayette County, KENTUCKY.

THE END.